# Uptight and In Your Face

# Uptight and In Your Face

*Coping with an Anxious Boss, Parent, Spouse, or Lover*

Nina W. Brown

PRAEGER

AN IMPRINT OF ABC-CLIO, LLC
Santa Barbara, California • Denver, Colorado • Oxford, England

**Library of Congress Cataloging-in-Publication Data**

Brown, Nina W.
  Uptight and in your face : coping with an anxious boss, parent, spouse, or lover / Nina W. Brown.
      p. cm.
  Includes bibliographical references and index.
  ISBN 978-0-313-38555-1 (hbk. : alk. paper) — ISBN 978-0-313-38556-8 (ebook) 1. Interpersonal conflict. 2. Interpersonal relations—Psychological aspects. 3. Personality assessment. 4. Stress (Psychology) 5. Adjustment (Psychology) I. Title. II. Title: Coping with an anxious boss, parent, spouse, or lover.
  BF637.I48B76   2011
  158.2—dc22        2010034546

ISBN: 978-0-313-38555-1
EISBN: 978-0-313-38556-8

15   14   13   12   11      1   2   3   4   5

This book is also available on the World Wide Web as an eBook.
Visit www.abc-clio.com for details.

Praeger
An Imprint of ABC-CLIO, LLC

ABC-CLIO, LLC
130 Cremona Drive, P.O. Box 1911
Santa Barbara, California 93116-1911

This book is printed on acid-free paper ∞

Manufactured in the United States of America

# Contents

# Acknowledgments

Appreciation and thanks are extended to many people who provided me with the inspiration for this book, and they shall remain nameless. However, some people deserve recognition for their support and encouragement during the writing process. I want to thank Hylene Dublin, MSW, for listening and understanding what I was trying to sort out and convey; George Saiger, MD, who always has good suggestions and gives encouragement; and Rosemary Thompson, Ed.D, a good friend and fellow writer.

Thanks are also extended to Debbie Carvalko, the editor at ABC-CLIO who guided me through this process and saw the potential for this book.

My heartfelt thanks go to each one of you.

Nina W. Brown
May 2010

# Preface

This book was written to be a guide and support for people who have to live, work, or interact on a regular basis with someone who is intense, anxious, and self-absorbed, which I term "uptight." The dictionary describes uptight as being tense, outraged, angry, and adhering rigidly to convention, but that definition only captures a part of what these people are like. Underlying the tenseness is anxiety, and yes, they do tend to be angry but it is difficult to know why they are angry or toward whom as their anger seems to be about and toward almost everything and everyone. Further, the rigid adherence is only for what they consider to be right and proper, with little or no understanding or adoption of standard conventions. In addition, the definition does not include mention of self-absorbed behaviors and attitudes that this book addresses.

This book grew out of my experiences with several people who were intense, anxious, and self-absorbed, but who did not or could not see or appreciate the negative impact of their attitudes and behaviors on others, and who would get very angry and defensive when I tried to make them aware of how they were affecting me and others. They were not able to understand that the relationships were affected, seemed to have an attitude that they were right, and that others just ought to accept the validity of what they said or did without having any negative feelings. They did not seem to care about others' feelings and perspectives, although they constantly said that they did, and were devaluing and dismissive of these.

In addition to these upsetting behaviors and attitudes, they seemed to have also some other characteristics in common that could be seen as obsessive and/or compulsive, but did not exhibit the understanding of someone with obsessive-compulsive disorder (OCD). Usually, people with OCD seem to understand that what they are doing is over the top, so to speak, but they are unable to stop or prevent this. In contrast, the people that I encountered and describe in this book tend to have an inner conviction that they are "right," and that "if others were more like them, the world would be a better place." The description of obsessive-compulsive personality disorder (OCPD) brought things into order and perspective for me, and I termed people who have some of these characteristics as uptight. While the people described in this book may or likely do not have OCPD, they can exhibit some of these behaviors and attitudes. (APA, 2000)

I try to explain their behaviors and attitudes, the impact of these on others who have to interact with them on a regular basis, and to suggest coping strategies. All of what is presented is intended to be as positive as possible with a major assumption that the uptight person is either oblivious to how others are negatively impacted by his/her behaviors and/or attitudes, or really believes that he/she is "right" and that others should be more like him/her.

# 1

# Intense, Anxious, and Self-Absorbed

When intensity, anxiety, and self-absorption are melded together in one person, the result is someone who has and exhibits numerous behaviors and attitudes that have negative impact on those who must interact with them on a regular basis. The extent of their uptightness is insular, wide, deep, and extensive. This book is written for people who have to interact with an uptight person, and will explore some of their characteristics and the behavioral manifestations of these, try to give a picture of their internal thoughts, feelings, and ideas that produce many of the distressing behaviors and attitudes, illustrate five possible types, and provide specific coping strategies for those who have to live, work, and/or interact with them on a regular basis. Attention is also given to self-examination and self-exploration to help identify the reader's similarities and differences with an uptight person, suggest possible reasons for why readers react as they do, and provide other suggestions for their personal development that can help them better cope with the uptight person in their life. We begin with two vignettes.

## The Micromanaging Boss

*Phil had worked hard on the report and felt that he had done a good job, although he had not been given the resources needed. He submitted the report, and two days later the boss's assistant called him and told him to come imme-diately to the boss's office. Phil wondered what this was about and hurried to the office. As he entered, the boss greeted him in a pleasant tone, and Phil began to relax. He even allowed himself to imagine that he had done such a* good job on the report that the boss had called him in to compliment him. After inquiring generally about how the work was going, the mood abruptly changed. The boss leaned forward, frowned, and told Phil that he was disappointed in the quality of the report he submitted and could not accept it as he, the boss, would look bad to the vice president for accepting such inferior work. Phil was very surprised and nonplussed, but he managed to ask the boss what was wrong with the report. The boss's voice boomed as he told Phil that he could not tolerate such sloppy, incompetent work. There were so many errors that he did not know where to start and did not have time to go over all of them with Phil. Phil tried to tell the boss that he would work to correct the errors, but the boss did not listen. He tossed the report on the desk, told Phil to take it and have it fixed in the next hour, or he would give it to someone else. Phil felt incompetent, inadequate, and humiliated because he knew that others had heard what the boss said as his voice was so loud.

Phil took the report back to his office and looked at the boss's comments and corrections. He became very angry when he saw that the boss's corrections and comments consisted of substituting semi-colons for some commas, marking that two bottom margins were wrong (they were a little over one inch), changed three words where either word would be correct, and noted one misspelled word. Phil read it three times, but these were the only comments noted. Nothing substantive was noted as needing changes. Phil did not understand the boss's reaction, which seemed excessive in light of what the boss noted as errors.

### The Hoarding Secretary

Betty had been in this new job for two months and was at her wits' end. She had tried for weeks to get the office organized so that she could find materials, understand the requirements for the position, and get the work done, but was being thwarted at every turn by her secretary, Rita. Rita had been in that position for about eight years, and the previous boss had let her do whatever she wanted to. Betty wanted to use Rita's expertise, but every time Betty tried to find out what Rita was doing, Rita managed to find some way to be unresponsive. For example, when Betty asked Rita to give her a list of the tasks she (Rita) needed to do that day so that Betty could help or re-prioritize tasks, Rita left, saying that she did not feel well. Betty never did find out what Rita was doing most days, as Betty had to attend many meetings related to her new position.

This uncommunicative behavior was only part of the concern. The office was overflowing with materials and supplies. Every drawer, cabinet, chair, desk, etc., was filled with materials and supplies. There was literally an 18-inch *pathway into Rita's office through piles of materials. Betty had asked why so many materials and supplies were needed, but Rita just shrugged and did not provide any real answers. Betty had set a goal of cleaning out the materials and supplies, and Rita said that she would, but nothing was done. Betty had talked with Rita several times, but no headway was being made, and Betty was frustrated.*

*Betty decided to talk with a colleague who knew Rita, and to ask for suggestions. What the colleague told her produced even more consternation. Rita not only hoarded materials and supplies at the office, but her home was full of them, and her family had to work their way around rooms of stuff as well as office supplies and materials. They were all over the place, and Rita never stopped accumulating more and more.*

The micromanaging boss is demonstrating at a minimum, a noticeable lack of empathy, shows no awareness of the impact of his behavior on Phil, is overreacting to minor mistakes and imperfections, is more concerned about his image with his bosses than the relationship with Phil, and demonstrates an entitlement attitude when he unloads his anxiety onto Phil.

The example with Rita illustrates an outcome for intensity, anxiety, and self-absorption that negatively impacts her relationships, the quality of her life, and her physical and emotional well-being. Rita has her life ordered to her needs, ignores or dismisses the needs of the other person in all relationships (even her most intimate ones), and cannot stop the self-destructive behavior.

While both the boss and Rita have issues and concerns that would be helpful for them to explore and understand in order to modify behavior, that task is beyond the scope of this book. What is the focus for this book are the people who, like Phil and Betty, encounter individuals like these on a regular basis; have or are suffering negative thoughts and feelings about their self, the person, and/or the relationship; and who have tried without success to effectively cope with the distressing effects of the person's intensity, anxiety, and self-absorption. Discussed are the following:

- Negative reactions experienced in an interaction, and the long-term effects on the relationship
- What other people see from the uptight person's behavior, such as disguised hostility, edginess, and startling actions
- The fears, chaos, and responses to uncertainty and ambiguity that exist in the uptight person's internal landscape

- Five general types: Hoarders, Misers, Indulgers, Sneaks, and Terrorists
- Some possible explanations for your reactions; why you voluntarily get involved with the person, why you stay in the relationship, when you feel trapped with no seemingly viable options for leaving (such as with a job), the need to recognize your fantasies and limitations, and so on
- Effective coping strategies to reduce negative impact on you, to build resistance and resiliency, set reasonable limits on intrusions into your personal physical and psychological space, and how to reduce the stress of continual interactions that are unsatisfying, demeaning, hostile, and/or manipulative

Embedded in most chapters are scales and exercises designed to assist readers' understanding, growth, and development. You are encouraged to complete these, and to reflect on your personal thoughts, feelings, and ideas that emerge during the process. Doing so can provide you with some self-awareness and self-understanding, and increases your understanding, awareness, and sensitivity toward others. You can learn how to protect yourself from incorporating projections from others, what personal characteristics you have that can be strengthened and enhanced, and other personal growth and development strategies. These are personal growth strategies that will help you to cope better with uptight people and to suffer fewer negative and distressing effects from interactions with them.

The material presented is based on the following assumptions:

- You are in a relationship—personal, work, or intimate—with someone who could be described as intense, anxious, and self-absorbed. You have numerous negative reactions to and about the person and are seeking ways to cope with your feelings and/or that person.
- You have tried numerous times to understand, be sympathetic or empathic with him/her, and to reduce the negative feelings and thoughts you experience, but your attempts have not been successful.
- You may even have tried confrontation or other means to try to get that person to make modest changes, to be less uptight, and to understand the negative impact of their behavior and attitudes on you and others, all to no avail.

- To date, you are probably unable to accept that your efforts to try and change another person will not work. You continue to try, but your efforts do not produce any desired results.
- The intense, anxious, and self-absorbed person is mired in a fear of destruction, lacks empathy and is indifferent to others' concerns, demonstrates undeveloped narcissism, assumes that others are as he/she is, and does not know of any other way of existing.
- You are seeking more effective ways to prevent the negative impact on you, to manage and contain your negative reactions and emotions, and to obtain hope that there can be a better relationship or situation.
- The uptight person has certain behaviors and attitudes reflective of his/her personality, of some psychological underdevelopment, and lags in expected growth of separation and individuation.

## A DESCRIPTION FOR INTENSE, ANXIOUS, AND SELF-ABSORBED

Intensity alone does not have to be negative. When someone is intense, he/she is focused, has concentrated energies, is able to screen out distractions, and being so helps in goal attainment. Just think about how you are when you are engaged in something of considerable interest to you, such as working on a hobby. Time passes without your awareness, you don't think about other things, and you don't let external things disrupt what you are doing. Other examples where intensity can be positive include athletes, performers, and those doing work they enjoy.

However, sustained intensity over time can have negative effects on the physical, emotional, and relational self. For example, there is considerable evidence that sustained intensity is stressful and produces physical effects, such as elevated blood pressure and other cardiac and vascular concerns, or even can produce medical disorders.

Anxiety, when it is intermittent, logical, and used as an early warning alert notification, also has some positive aspects. For example, becoming anxious in a potentially dangerous situation can allow you to take steps to remain safe. Another example could be seen when someone reduces spending because of anxiety over a pending financial situation. However, anxiety can also be so negative as to prevent logical and reasonable thoughts, decisions, judgments, and actions; to paralyze the person so that he/she remains stuck in an untenable situation, to act in inappropriate and even dangerous ways, and other self-defeating reactions and outcomes. Anxious people worry excessively even when there is nothing substantial in their world to produce the worry; they fret over inconsequential matters, fantasize possible dangers to the self that demand their constant alertness, remain tense and edgy, and expend considerable energy and effort on remaining safe. They stay in a constant state of fearing abandonment and destruction.

Self-absorbed adults have an excessive self-focus and self-interest that is seen in their behaviors and attitudes that reflect an inflated and impoverished self, indifference to others and their concerns, and an inability to perceive the negative impact they have on others. In short, they have considerable undeveloped narcissism in that they do not have a strong and complete sense of their self as separate and distinct from others; they have an excessive focus on their concerns and needs, with insufficient thought or appreciation for others' concerns and needs; and they have not yet sufficiently developed healthy adult narcissism. Undeveloped narcissism and healthy adult narcissism are explained more fully in the next section. This presentation is limited to a brief description to show it in proximity to intensity and anxiety so that readers can begin to get a deeper understanding of uptight as presented in this book.

Self-absorption is not self-care, which can be a positive characteristic. Caring for oneself can be necessary and appropriate. But, when the self is the center of all or most all thoughts and efforts, others are not perceived as separate and distinct individuals who are also worthwhile and valued. There is a noticeable lack of empathy in almost all interactions and relationships, and few emotions are experienced or expressed except for anger, and then the care for oneself is excessive and is self-absorptive. This is what is described and meant as narcissistic much of the time, and is not necessarily as extreme or intense as is the psychiatric diagnosis of Narcissistic Personality Disorder.

## IDENTIFYING THE UPTIGHT INDIVIDUAL

Did the brief description in the previous section seem to fit someone you know? Use the following exercise and rate that person on these items.

**Exercise 1.1**

**The Uptight Identification Scale**

*Directions:* Think of someone with whom you interact on a regular basis who you think is intense, anxious, and self-absorbed; and whose attitudes and behaviors are troubling to your relationship with him/her. Use the following scale to rate the person:

> 5–Always or almost always; extremely
> 4–Very frequently; very much; considerably
> 3–Often; frequently
> 2–Sometimes; infrequently; seldom
> 1–Never or almost never

1. Gets upset when things do not go as planned or as he/she desires.     5 4 3 2 1

2. Expects others to keep things in order and also in line with his/her definition for order.     5 4 3 2 1

3. Is thrown off balance by surprising or unpredictable minor events.     5 4 3 2 1

4. Demands and expects perfection for self.     5 4 3 2 1

5. Demands and expects perfection for others.     5 4 3 2 1

6. Micromanages to ensure that mistakes are not made, that things are done as he/she want them done, and/or does not delegate work or tasks.     5 4 3 2 1

7. Does not easily accept or adjust to even minor changes.     5 4 3 2 1

8. Overindulges self (e.g. eating, alcohol use, spending, and so on)     5 4 3 2 1

9. Is constantly "on the go"; displays lots of physical movement.     5 4 3 2 1

10. Cannot relax.     5 4 3 2 1

11. Spends excessive time with attention to details.     5 4 3 2 1

12. Becomes upset when others differ or disagree with him/her; perceives disagreements as threats or danger.     5 4 3 2 1

13. Will not accept or admit any personal failings or mistakes.     5 4 3 2 1

14. Excessively consumed with work, spends long hours with work-related concerns.     5 4 3 2 1

15. Indifferent to the needs and/or rights of others.     5 4 3 2 1

16. Exploits others, e.g. takes advantage of someone's
    good nature for his/her benefit.                    5 4 3 2 1

17. Expects understanding from others but does not
    reciprocate.                                        5 4 3 2 1

18. Seeks attention and/or admiration.                  5 4 3 2 1

19. Can be rigid, intolerant, and unyielding.           5 4 3 2 1

20. Judgmental and dismissive of others.                5 4 3 2 1

Scoring: Add the ratings and use the following as a guide.

| Score | Guide |
|-------|-------|
| 85–100 | Extremely intense, anxious, and self-absorbed |
| 69–84 | Very intense, anxious, and self-absorbed |
| 53–68 | Demonstrates moderate intensity, anxiety, and self-absorption |
| 37–52 | Somewhat intense, anxious, and self-absorbed at times |
| 20–36 | Seldom, if ever, intense, anxious, and self-absorbed |

**Explanation of Scoring**

*Extreme (85–100).* The person rated high on the scale exhibits most all of the attitudes and behaviors descriptive of being intense, anxious, and self-absorbed. It is likely that the person does not have enduring and satisfying long-term intimate relationships, acts in ways that are destructive to relationships and to the self-esteem of others, may be very successful at work because of excessive time commitments and attention to details for the job, others find it uncomfortable to be around him/her, the person has a noticeable lack of empathy, and usually makes quick and rigid judgments about others.

*Very (69–84).* This level is less than the previous one, but there can be some extreme intense, anxious, and self-absorbed behaviors and attitudes, just not as many, and some may be less intense. While people rated at this level can have some enduring relationships, these tend not to be satisfying or meaningful. They exhibit edginess, an excessive need for perfection from self and from others, have the correct words for empathic responding but these are not accompanied by the appropriate feelings, exploits others for their own personal benefit, and values predictability and control.

*Moderate (53–68).* Ratings in this category are descriptive of people who can be extreme or very intense, anxious, and self-absorbed at times, and/or for some of those behaviors and attitudes. They are not so all of the time, as are people rated in the previous two categories.

*Somewhat, at times (37–52).* Ratings at this level describe people who can occasionally be intense and anxious and self-absorbed, but usually exhibit one or the other, but not all three categories. For example, they can be anxious about an impending event, but not necessarily intense, or self-absorbed.

*Seldom, if ever (20–36).* These ratings are descriptive of someone who can be intense at times, anxious at times, has some undeveloped narcissism, but only in certain areas, and very infrequently or never exhibits all of these at the same time.

The material in the rest of this book is intended to present information that relates to individuals rated 50 or higher, and who have significant numbers of the behaviors and attitudes that describe the uptight person. We now turn to describing some of the impact the uptight person can have on others and on their relationships,

## THE IMPACT OF UPTIGHT PEOPLE

First, some reactions will be described, and then the impact on relationships. You may have experienced several of the following reactions to the person(s) you identified as uptight:

- Feel tense, nervous, and/or anxious when in their presence, especially when you are with them for any amount of time.
- Try hard to understand their feelings and perspective without success, or without reciprocity.
- Experience feelings of inadequacy, incompetency, and/or of not being good enough.
- Stay alert to try to capture their nuances of feelings so that you can try to please them.
- Feel diminished and dismissed if you try to talk about any of your concerns with them.
- Can experience shame and guilt feelings as you realize that they feel you are failing them.

- Feel despair that you cannot fully please them.
- Experience chaotic and/or fragmented thoughts and feelings when in their presence, and these can linger for you.
- Can feel anger, frustration, and even rage.
- Feel hopeless and helpless, especially when you don't have other reasons for feeling this way.

These are some of the more distressing feelings that can be experienced in interactions with someone who is uptight, especially when there are sustained and frequent interactions, such as those that can happen with a boss, friend, parent, lover, or spouse. Your responses to these feelings can be to rationalize or try to minimize them, to get away from the person, or even to incorporate and act on the feelings. Ways that you can act on them include becoming less empathic with others, being tense and anxious without understanding why, or feeling despair or anger. You may not be able to identify what is happening, you just know that you are upset and uncomfortable, and you try to get rid of these feelings quickly. There is information in every chapter that tries to explain what may be happening to you, and chapters nine and ten are focused on explaining and presenting additional coping strategies.

What are some impacts on the relationship? Included are the following:

- You avoid interactions that include the uptight person because of the discomfort experienced in his/her presence.
- You try to avoid spending a considerable amount of time with the person.
- You find yourself zoning out or drifting off when talking with him/her.
- You and others can feel criticized, blamed, minimized, or dismissed by their actions, words, and attitudes.
- You can experience feelings of frustration and inadequacy because this person's needs cannot be fully anticipated or met no matter how much effort is expended.
- You "get it wrong" much of the time.
- This person's needs are central almost always, and other's needs are subjugated.
- Your opinions are not valued, or are thought to be disagreements, and therefore are wrong.

- You feel dread and discomfort before, during and after interactions with them because of their edginess and anxiety, But you may not be able to identify what is causing these feelings.

A strong and persistent theme that runs through the impact of the uptight person on relationships is avoidance. Avoidance is seen in a reluctance to engage with him/her; minimizing time spent in their presence; keeping away from topics that arouses their ire, blame, or criticism; a careful choice of words so as to not offend, and thus a reduction of genuineness; and a resistance to intimacy. The feelings aroused for you lead to wariness, tentativeness, and other self-protective strategies. It's difficult to feel warm, caring, or even loving under these conditions. But, every relationship has its unique set of characteristics and expectations. Discussed next are the behaviors and attitudes of the uptight boss or supervisor, a parent, or a spouse or lover.

## THE UPTIGHT BOSS

Uptight bosses are probably very successful in their chosen field, career, or job. This success has come as a result of their excessive dedication to the work, and for some, work has consumed so much of their time and energy that they have little remaining for self-care, relationships, or socialization apart from their work. Their intensity and anxiety fuel their excessive attention to details. They work hard to attain perfection, and may do most of the work him/herself for fear that others will not meet his/her standards for perfection. No matter how hard others try to meet their standards, they cannot because these are unrealistic and overly demanding.

Other behaviors and attitudes that the uptight boss can exhibit are reflective of self-absorption. These can include many of the following:

- Take unearned credit for work that others do, and/or fail to acknowledge others' contributions
- Insist that things be done his/her way, and can be inflexible and rigid even about trivial things of little or no importance
- Shows little or no understanding of others' perspectives, concerns, or needs
- Constantly seeks attention and/or admiration
- Has favorite workers that are approved of and accepted more than are others

- Finds it difficult or impossible to delegate tasks or responsibilities
- Does not manage change well; can be rigid and inflexible
- Can be quick to take offense, tends to hold grudges, and expects total agreement with his/her perspective

These are some behaviors and attitudes that can reflect self-absorption. When these are combined with intensity and anxiety, they can produce a boss who has a strong and negative impact on many who work for and with him/her. This person's achievements can outweigh all other concerns for those who are his/her bosses. Their negative impact on other workers and their peers can be ignored or minimized because of this focus on outcomes. Some of the most troubling behaviors and attitudes of uptight bosses can be hidden from their superiors because the uptight boss presents and reacts to the superiors differently than they do with subordinates and peers, and/or because their superiors share may or some of the same characteristics and they do not see the problem with these.

## THE UPTIGHT PARENT

Uptight parents can communicate and transmit their intensity and anxiety to their children, and can also put the children in the position of experiencing many of the negative effects of parentification, or reverse parenting. Parentification occurs when the child does not receive the level of nurturing needed for psychological growth and development, such as what can happen when the parent frequently or consistently fails to empathize with the child. In addition, the child is expected to fulfill the parent's needs, especially their emotional needs. This is reverse of expected parenting, as expected parenting would have the parent empathizing, nurturing, and taking care of the child's needs. Negative effects of the self-absorbed parent on the child can result in the following for that child as he/she becomes an adult:

- An inability to tolerate intimacy, or a tendency to want to get too close and be fused or enmeshed with others
- A defiant attitude with little concern about pleasing others, or an excessive need to please others sometimes at the expense of oneself
- Decreased self-confidence, self-efficacy, and self-esteem
- An overemphasis on trying to please others, even when they do not have the responsibility for others' well-being

- Engage in behaviors that can be self-destructive because of manipulation by others

These are only a few of the possible outcomes for children with a parent who has a Destructive Narcissistic Pattern (Brown, 2001). This parent can exhibit some of the following behaviors and attitudes:

- The child is an extension of the parent, under the parent's control, and is only loved and approved of when the child meets the parent's needs and expectations.
- The child is expected to take care of the parent's feelings, but does not receive empathy from the parent.
- The parent thinks that all accomplishments by the child are due to the parent's efforts, expertise, and so on, but any failures, mistakes, and the like, are the child's fault.
- The parent is never wrong about anything.
- The child is expected to read the parent's mind, know what the parent wants and needs, and to act to see to it that the parent gets this without the parent having to ask or verbalize it.

Again, remember that these are only some of the troubling behaviors and attitudes of a self-absorbed parent. Add to these the intensity and anxiety that are a part of the uptight person's description, and you find a parent who is always on edge, expects the worst and constantly worries about fantasized disasters, can never relax or let those around him/her relax, has unrealistic demands for perfection by the child, does not meet the nurturing needs of the child and seems indifferent or oblivious to these needs, and a situation where all family energies revolve around that parent. Growing up with an uptight parent is unsettling, uncomfortable, and can produce a void for feelings, both for awareness and for expression, and make it difficult for the adult child to form and maintain meaningful, satisfying and enduring relationships. The adult can have a sense that something is wrong or missing, but not understand what or why.

## THE UPTIGHT INTIMATE PARTNER

The troubling part of being in an intimate relationship with an uptight partner is the unexpectedness of the negative behaviors and attitudes he/she displays. You either did not see these before you became so involved, you minimized and rationalized those you did observe, or he/she was able to successfully conceal them. You probably found that you were surprised at some of your partner's reactions and/or behavior, examples of which include:

- Constant nagging and chastising for not doing things "right," even small things of little or no consequence
- Becoming overly upset when things don't go as planned, and not getting over it
- Unable to tolerate surprises, and wanting to know and/or plan every detail
- Expecting you to do things his/her way, and getting upset when you do not
- Pushing you to be more like him/her
- Exhibiting inflexibility, rigidity, and stubbornness
- Not easily forgiving mistakes, neither his/hers nor those of others
- Not being satisfied with "just good enough" for anything, and being disappointed when you are satisfied with less than perfection
- Displaying a lack of empathy for you when he/she feels you should or ought to have known better, or acted differently; failing to see or value your perspective

There are other examples that could be described, but these are sufficient to illustrate some behaviors and attitudes of the uptight intimate partner.

The relationship is usually negatively affected because you cannot live up to their exacting standards no matter how hard you try, and their self-absorption can mean that your needs are not met, their understanding and empathy are inadequate, and you stay on edge, constantly expecting something unpleasant because you are open to catching his/her intensity and anxiety. When you allow yourself to be aware of the negative impacts on you and on the relationship, you may try to discuss these or confront your partner. What is likely to happen may then include the following:

- Your words and actions are turned back on you.
- Your deficiencies and shortcomings, as he/she perceives these, are listed in detail to illustrate how you are inadequate.
- His/her fortitude in putting up with you is magnified. (After all, he/she doesn't fail to live up to standards as you fail to do.)

- There is no acknowledgment or understanding of your feelings in the discussion.
- You leave the interaction feeling worse than when you began it, and you didn't think that was possible.

It may take considerable time before you accept that confrontation does not work, or you may still be trying it in the hope of getting through to him/her. I hate to tell you this, but confrontation did not work, is not working, and will not work. Your partner is impervious to confrontation as he/she has a deeply held conviction that he/she is 'right' or correct. You may need to try other ways to feel more adequate, to be less hurt when criticized and blamed, and learn new ways to cope.

The most important decision is whether to remain in the relationship or not. This book does not advocate for either position as you are the best judge of what will be best for you. What it does describe are ways to cope and build yourself, to understand the uptight intimate partner better, to learn what you want in and from a relationship, and to identify your possible self-absorbed behavior and attitudes. (Yes, you too may have some undeveloped narcissism.)

## BRIEF OVERVIEW OF THE BOOK

Chapter 1 sets the stage for what is presented by describing the general behaviors, attitudes, and characteristics of the uptight person and the negative impact on relationships, and introduces the discussion about the uptight person as the boss, as a parent, and as an intimate partner.

Chapter 2 expands the descriptions for the behaviors and attitudes, providing examples and illustrations. Also provided are exercises designed to explore the impact on you, and on the relationship.

Chapter 3 provides some insight into the uptight person's internal landscape. Possible explanations are provided for their lack of empathy, attacking and aggressive behavior, and their inability to perceive others as separate and distinct worthwhile individuals of value.

Chapters 4 through 8 describe five types: Impoverished Hoarders, Spartan and Withholding, Indulgent and Entitled, Controlling and Manipulative, and the Revengeful Complainer. These chapters also provide some possible coping strategies based on type.

Chapter 9 focuses on self-understanding. Explored are your reactions, how to recognize and accept your limitations, and how to build psychological boundary strength to cope with the negative effects and impact of sustained interactions with uptight people. Chapter 10 presents general coping strategies for various situations, such as conflicts, and for moderating the negative effects on you and on the relationship.

# 2

# What You See and Feel

## INTRODUCTION

Presented in this chapter are scales and exercises designed to sort through the myriad of perceptions and feelings about the uptight person, and to help identify the pattern of behaviors and attitudes for the person you designate as uptight. This is followed by an expanded description of self-absorbed behaviors and attitudes. Interspersed are suggestions for coping with these behaviors, attitudes, and triggered feelings for the characteristics of intense and anxious.

Chapter 1 presented a description of the uptight person, and this chapter continues that description with explanations and illustrations for some behaviors that you and others can observe, and that will have a negative impact on relationships. This focus on external behavior is provided because you cannot know uptight people's thoughts, ideas, or attitudes. Even when they seem to express these, you can only know what you observe. And even that can be misleading, because your interpretation is influenced by your internal state, past history and experiences, and unresolved issues and concerns. However, you can observe their behavior and try to be somewhat objective.

Let's begin this chapter with a short exercise that focuses on your conscious and unconscious perceptions and feelings about the uptight person in your life.

### Exercise 2.1
### Images and Feelings
*Materials*: A set of crayons, felt markers, or colored pencils for drawing, two or more sheets of unlined paper, and a pen or pencil for writing.

*Procedure*: Find a place to work where you will not be disturbed. This place should have a suitable surface for drawing and writing.

1. Sit in silence and think about the uptight person you know. Don't try to edit the thoughts, feelings, and images that emerge, just let them come and note what they are. Take as much time as you wish to get as much information about this person as you perceive him/her.
2. When your visualization seems complete, open your eyes and use your materials to draw symbols for the following. Symbols can be realistic or abstract.
   • A symbol that captures the essence of how you perceive the person.
   • A symbol for his/her most troubling behavior toward you.
   • A symbol for his/her most troubling attitude toward you.
   • A symbol or symbols for your feelings about the person. You may have several feelings, and try to capture all of these.
3. Take another sheet of paper and a pen or pencil. Look at the symbols you drew and write a summary statement or paragraph about your drawings. You can write as much as you wish, but try to summarize the drawings.
4. Review what you wrote, and make a short list of any feelings and other associations that come to mind as you read your review.

You now have an overview of your perception of the uptight person, his/her most troubling behaviors and attitudes, and the impact of these on you as seen in your feelings that you listed. The rest of the chapter will be focused on helping you understand what and how the intensity, anxiety, and self-absorption is displayed in overt and covert ways, and suggestions to cope with some of these so as to reduce the negative impact on you.

Let's begin with identifying some behaviors that could be indicative of the intense, anxious, and self-absorbed person. We want to determine **if these form a pattern,** the frequency to which these are exhibited significantly, and/or if they are extreme. That is, these are not isolated behaviors that appear infrequently, and/or are not deeply ingrained as a part of the person. A pattern means that there are numerous such behaviors, they occur frequently, and seem to be a part of the person. There are separate scales to assess intensity, anxiety, and self-absorption. Rate someone you think could be characterized as uptight on each of the three scales. After completing the three scales, you will be asked to combine the separate scale ratings to assess the level and **extent** to which the person could be termed uptight.

**Exercise 2.2**

**Intensity Scale**

Directions: Rate the person on each of the following items using the scale:

> 5–Always or almost always;
> 4–Frequently;
> 3–Sometimes;
> 2–Seldom; and
> 1–Never or almost never

| | |
|---|---|
| 1. Alert and on guard, edgy | 5 4 3 2 1 |
| 2. Has difficulty with resting, sleeping, and/or relaxing | 5 4 3 2 1 |
| 3. Can be a bully | 5 4 3 2 1 |
| 4. "Sweats the small stuff" | 5 4 3 2 1 |
| 5. Holds on to grudges, perceived and/or imagined slights, criticisms, and the like | 5 4 3 2 1 |
| 6. Has numerous physical complaints/concerns/ disorders | 5 4 3 2 1 |
| 7. Whines, carps, complains, kvetches | 5 4 3 2 1 |
| 8. Is easily panicked, and assumes the worst | 5 4 3 2 1 |
| 9. Tends to look for, and focus on, what is "wrong" | 5 4 3 2 1 |
| 10. Focused and not easily distracted | 5 4 3 2 1 |

Scoring: Add the ratings to derive a total score.

43–50: Extremely intense; displayes these behaviors and attitudes always or almost always

35–42: Very intense: very frequently displays these behaviors and attitudes

27–34: Somewhat intense: will display these behaviors and attitudes many times

19–26: Can be intense sometimes: infrequently displays the behaviors and attitudes

10–18: Seldom or never intense

*Intense.* Scores 35 and above can indicate intensity that is extreme or bordering on extreme. The person with these scores displays a concentrated level of energy that is somewhat reflective of stress. They put themselves and others in a constant state where relaxation is difficult or impossible. They have an internal pressure to act, be in motion whether the motion is physical or mental, survey their world for possible and hidden dangers, and are very detail-oriented. Intense people can wonder why others are not as alert as they are, and insist or goad others into becoming as stressed as they are. Scores below 35 indicate lower levels or infrequent displays of intensity.

## Exercise 2.3 Anxiety Scale

*Directions*: Rate the person on each of the following items using the scale:

>            5–Always or almost always;
>            4–Frequently;
>            3–Sometimes;
>            2–Seldom; and
>            1–Never or almost never

1. Demands order, control, perfection for self
   and for others                                         5  4  3  2  1

2. Little flexibility or adjustment to change             5  4  3  2  1

3. Becomes upset when others are not consistent
   or predictable                                         5  4  3  2  1

4. Expects the worst; looks for possible disasters        5  4  3  2  1

5. Overly inflates adversity, or adverse
   circumstances                                          5  4  3  2  1

6. Wants to do things his/her way                         5  4  3  2  1

7. Uncomfortable and impatient with collabora-
   tion, but can fake it                                  5  4  3  2  1

8. Exhibits unexpected hostility when faced with
   disagreements or challenges                            5  4  3  2  1

9. Can display vindictiveness and/or meanness             5  4  3  2  1

10. Micromanages                                          5  4  3  2  1

Scoring: Add the ratings to derive a total score.

43–50: Always or almost always displays the behaviors and/or attitudes

35–42: Very frequently displays the behaviors and/or attitudes

27–34: Frequently displays the behaviors and/or attitudes

19–26: Sometimes displays the behaviors and/or attitudes

10–18: Never or almost never displays the behaviors and/or attitudes

*Anxious.* Items on this scale describe some of the behaviors and attitudes that can be reflective of this person's attempts to relieve the constant anxiousness they experience. Their anxiety can arise from fears of abandonment and/or destruction, perceived inadequacies, and shame for imagined and real flaws. Their fears may not be recognized as such, but still continue to exert influence on the person, who then strives to try and ensure that their inner fears, perceptions, and shame are not recognized by others. Scores of 35 and above can indicate constant acts to address their anxiety, suggesting that they are very anxious. Scores below 35 suggest modest anxiety at times.

**Exercise 2.4**

**Self-absorption Scale**

*Directions*: Rate the person on each of the following items using the scale:

> 5–Always or almost always;
> 4–Frequently;
> 3–Sometimes;
> 2–Seldom; and
> 1–Never or almost never

1. Quick to take offense at perceived slights, blame, and/or criticism  5 4 3 2 1

2. Self-protective and self-focused in conversations and interactions  5 4 3 2 1

3. Demands and expects your immediate attention  5 4 3 2 1

4. Becomes angry and upset when you don't drop everything because he/she wants your attention  5 4 3 2 1

5. Finds it difficult to assume another person's perspective  5 4 3 2 1

6. Can respond with the proper words but not
   with empathy                                        5 4 3 2 1

7. Boasts, brags, inflates accomplishments             5 4 3 2 1

8. Blames, criticizes, and/or minimizes others and
   their accomplishments                               5 4 3 2 1

9. Says depreciating things about almost everyone      5 4 3 2 1

10. Is disappointed when others do not meet his/
    her exacting standards and makes comments
    about his/her disappointment                       5 4 3 2 1


Scoring: Add the ratings and derive a total score

43–50: Displays numerous self-absorbed behaviors and attitudes almost all of the time

35–42: Displays many self-absorbed behaviors and attitudes much of the time

27–34: Sometimes displays some self-absorbed behaviors and attitudes

19–26: Can display some self-absorbed behaviors and/or attitudes, but does so infrequently

10–18: Never or almost never displays self-absorbed behaviors and/or attitudes

*Self-absorbed.* The behaviors and attitudes on this scale are descriptions that can be categorized as self-absorbed, and illustrate the impoverished self that is fearful and self-depreciating while at the same time is grandiose, hyperaware and sensitive to hints of criticism from external sources, is attention-seeking, does not have a clear sense of others as separate and distinct from him/her, demonstrates a lack of empathy, and is admiration-seeking, arrogant, and contemptuous. Scores of 35 and above indicate considerable self-absorbed behaviors and attitudes most of the time. Scores below 35 indicate some of these some of the time.

## TOTAL SCORES FOR UPTIGHT DESIGNATIONS

You now have scores for the person on intensity, anxiety and self-absorption. Since the designation as uptight includes all three categories, it is necessary to add the scores for all three scales.

Intensity scale score      _____
Anxiety scale score      _____
Self-absorption scale score _____

Use the following groupings to determine the level and extent to which the person is uptight.

127–150      Extremely uptight
103–126      Very uptight
79–102      Somewhat uptight
55–78      Can be mostly intense, anxious, or self-absorbed, but not all three much of the time
30–54      Few, if any, observable behaviors reflective of being uptight

## 127–150 Extremely Uptight

This person is the poster child for the definition of uptight used in this book. He/she is a "bundle of nerves," constantly on edge, and has a significant number of self-absorbed behaviors and attitudes. This person is inflexible; rigid about his/her version of ethical behavior, moral standards, and values; and this personal version may not be related to culture or religion. They can be stubborn and unforgiving; would describe him/herself as overly conscientious; may be very successful at work; and has few or no enjoyable pursuits or friends.

The extremely uptight person can have numerous physical conditions and illnesses such as ulcers, hypertension, kidney problems, nervous system malfunctions, circulatory system problems, asthma, angina, and gastrointestinal problems. It could be that their efforts to try to control their external and internal worlds exact a toll on their bodies.

A noticeable behavior is their inability to relax, rest, and/or sleep. They may have periods where they are able to slow down, but these periods tend to cause more stress rather than relieving it. Their eternal vigilance could be similar to that experienced in combat situations where the person is constantly in danger of destruction. However, the body needs rest for optimal health and functioning, and the inability to rest could contribute to the physical complaints. (Self-absorbed behaviors and attitudes will be addressed more fully in a separate section after the discussion about the total score.)

## 103–126 Very Much Intense, Anxious, and Self-Absorbed

An extensive explanation was presented for scores falling into the extreme category. People who are rated in the category of very much, display many of the same behaviors as do those rated in the extreme category, but have fewer such behaviors or they don't occur as often. This person can still be designated as uptight, but somewhat less so at times than someone designated as extremely so.

## 79–102 Somewhat Intense, Anxious, and Self-Absorbed

People whose ratings fall into this category exhibit fewer intense, anxious, and self-absorbed behaviors than those whose ratings are in the previous two categories, but these can still be designated as uptight behaviors. They exhibit some intensity, can act anxiously on occasion, and they have some self-absorbed behaviors.

## 55–78 Seldom Intense, Anxious, and Self-Absorbed

Ratings in this category are descriptive of people who are generally not intense, anxious, and self-absorbed all or much of the time. They can be intense or anxious or self-absorbed much of the time, exhibit behaviors that fall into the other two categories some of the time, but less so than those in the previous category.

## 30–54 Rarely Uptight

There are few of the described behaviors, and they are infrequent enough so that these people would not be designated as uptight.


## THE DOMINANT CATEGORY

Return to your scoring that indicates the dominant category: intense, anxious, or self-absorbed. (The highest score for the three categories designate that person's dominant category.) Note the category that is dominant for your designated uptight person. It may be helpful to try and understand it. That is, does he/she tend to be mostly intense, anxious, or self-absorbed. Refer back to the total rating for these categories. Understanding the dominant category can help you find creative ways to respond and cope. For example, if the person's dominant category falls into *Intense*, then you can become aware of how you may be catching and acting on his/her intensity, and then use strategies such as those described in chapters nine and ten to block the catching, which then prevents you from becoming intense and acting on it.

*Coping strategies.* Using the items listed on the scale as a guide, you can do the following to cope with the *Intense* individual:

- Don't keep trying to fix their physical symptoms as these are a part of their intensity. You may have noticed that these, or some of them, may be better for a period of time, but they never completely disappear.
- Accept that you will be either unable to distract this person, or only minimally so, and only infrequently. He/she is harder to deflect than a heat-seeking missile.
- Refrain from being logical and rational by suggesting that what they are fretting over is trivial or unimportant. They can't help it, and you only irritate or hurt them when you try to help them see a bigger picture or a different perspective.
- Sympathize and do what you can or need to do about their physical complaints. Don't do too much or suggest alternatives to try.
- Get your rest and relaxation elsewhere.
- Develop strong and resilient boundaries so that you will not be bullied by this person.

When the dominant category is *Anxious,* this person is trying to gain control over his/her inner world, and over the external environment. Intellectually, he/she may have achieved some understanding that control over much of the external world is not possible, but cannot stop trying to exert control. Their inner world is probably not well understood or accepted as the major source for their anxiety, nor can they exercise adequate control over their thoughts, feelings, ideas, and so on. Adequate in this sense means that person's definition of adequate. These people can never feel safe and secure, but continue to try to achieve this by excessive control of their external world.

*Coping strategies.* This insecurity fuels many of their reactions and behaviors such as hostility when others disagree with him/her, micro-managing, demands for order and perfection for self and for others, and exhibiting rigidity with little or no flexibility. Use the scale presented earlier in the chapter as a guide for which reactions and behaviors are most prevalent and/or troubling for you, and try to do things like the following. You can probably think of other ways to cope.

- Accept that you cannot provide sufficient reassurance to eliminate or prevent that person's anxiety. Become comfortable with providing some reassurance on occasion when you desire, but let the person have his/her anxiety.
- Compromise sometimes, but not always, on doing things his/her way.
- If he/she tends to micromanage, try to get directions and instructions in writing, and provide timely feedback on your progress. Feedback can be by e-mail, telephone, or a formal memo. Accept that the person is more comfortable and less likely to interrupt or bug you when he/she knows what is going on.
- When change is necessary, try to make it gradually and not abruptly.
- Restrict discussion of possibilities or alternatives as these can be anxiety producing. These people tend to fantasize disaster, and do not want to move or act because of this fear.
- Don't overreact to their unexpected hostility if you disagree with them, or when they are mean. Do not confront; just make a neutral comment or reaction and then leave their presence.
- Maintain your integrity as a separate and distinct person; know when you've given enough and feel adequate, and understand and accept your personal limitations.

*Coping strategies.* If the dominant category is *Self-absorbed*, there is nothing you can do that will cause the person to change. Self-absorption is addressed in more detail in the next section, and some more coping strategies are suggested in later chapters. For this section, recommended are the following:

- Give up the fantasy that you can do or say something that will cause them to change, or to want to change. They don't see any need to change, do not agree with you, and have not or will not change to please you.
- Use the emotional insulation strategies presented later in the book to prevent catching their strong negative emotions.
- Do not expect empathy from this person. That either will not happen, or is very unlikely to happen.

The next section presents an extended discussion of self-absorbed behaviors and attitudes to try and illustrate some of their abstract complexity. Many of the behaviors and attitudes are unconscious and the person simply cannot see these in him/herself which makes it futile to try and get them to change.

## SELF-ABSORPTION

Self-absorption for adults is defined here as an excessive self-focus with significant areas of undeveloped narcissism. These are inter-twined, but are not exactly the same. Undeveloped narcissism is defined as delayed development of some parts of self that result in behavior and attitudes reflective of earlier infant, child, and adoles-cent stages of development, and these behaviors and attitudes can negatively impact relationships in significant ways.

The self-absorbed behaviors discussed are an extreme self-focus, a lack of empathy, attention and admiration seeking, and grandiosity and its flip side, the impoverished ego. What follows are examples for these behaviors, but not the full range of such behaviors.

An *extreme self-focus* can be seen in the following:

- Conversations tend to be about his/her concerns, and even when conversations don't begin being about him/her, somehow these always turn to being about that person.
- Quick defenses are mounted by the uptight person when he/she feels criticized, attacked, shamed, or diminished.
- His/her feelings are more important in an interaction than are the other person's.
- He/she makes decisions involving others without consulting them.
- He/she sulks when he/she doesn't get his/her way for almost everything.

You may feel that someone is self-absorbed, or even have had that charge leveled against you, but you have not been able to identify what was done or said that produced the feeling or charge.

Your biggest challenge may be to cope with your triggered feelings as these are what you carry with you, and you can find them difficult to relinquish. Even when you are able to suppress, rationalize, or even forget them for periods of time, they return and can become even more distressful because you did not resolve them. In addition, there can be more incidents that trigger the same feelings and these accumulate and build over time. The impact of the uptight person's behaviors and attitudes on you can be very strong and very stressful. Following is a mindfulness exercise that may help you let go or moderate some distressful feelings, but is not intended to be an answer for why your feelings get triggered, or to prevent this from happening. The exercise is a stopgap measure that can provide some short term relief. The technique could also be helpful for any distress you experience as you read this book and reflect on the uptight person in your life.

**Exercise 2.5**
**Distress Relief**
*Materials*: None

*Procedure*: Find a place that is free from distractions and disruptions where you can sit in silence for 10–15 minutes. Read the procedure through before starting. The time you can devote to practicing mindfulness is not important, just use the time you have.

1.  Sit in silence with your eyes closed. If this doesn't feel right to you, sit with your eyes open. As you sit in silence, concentrate on your breathing and try to make it deep and even. This may take some effort on your part, but try and persist. Deeper breathing is calming.
2.  Once your breathing becomes deeper and more even, allow an image of an event or situation that triggered your anger to emerge. It doesn't have to be an event or situation with an uptight person, it can be some other incident, even one that occurred when you were a child. Mentally rate the intensity of your anger at this point as you recall the event, from 0 (no intensity) to 10 (extreme intensity).
3.  Recall the event in as much detail as possible, and once you have an image that captures the essence of the event for you, allow that image to pass before you like you were watching clouds in the sky move by, or as if you were sitting in a moving car and seeing the image as scenery outside. Parts of the image emerge, but are gone as the car or cloud moves on. Try not to stop the image, just let it pass on. If you think about the incident or about your feelings, just let these emerge, observe them without evaluating them, and let them also move through like clouds or scenery. Don't stop the car- or sky-watching. Stay with this as long as you can.
4.  When you are ready, open your eyes, recall the event or situation, and rate the intensity of your anger at this point from 0 (no

intensity) to 10 (extreme intensity). If your anger has a rating of 3 or above, repeat the breathing and imaging. Try to do this exercise until your intensity rating is 2 or less.

You may find that this exercise has changed your feeling even though the situation has remained the same. You no longer have the same distress. Moderating your feelings is what you can work to achieve, since it is unlikely that you will be able to change another person. Further, changing your feelings can impact the situation in some ways. This exercise worked on one feeling (anger), and you can try this exercise for other distress feelings you experience.

## IDENTIFYING SELF-ABSORBED BEHAVIORS AND ATTITUDES

It may be helpful to describe the behaviors and attitudes that reflect undeveloped narcissism which, in turn, can produce behaviors and attitudes that suggest self-absorption, or an excessive self-focus. Everyone will not display all of these, but can display a considerable number of them. You may also want to reflect on which of these descriptions fit you. Discussed briefly are attention seeking, admiration hungry, lack of empathy, emptiness at the core of oneself, an inappropriate sense of humor, shallow emotions, grandiosity with arrogance and contempt, an impoverished ego, exploitation of others, extensions of self, entitlement, and envy. More about these self-absorbed behaviors and attitudes appear in other chapters in the book.

Read these descriptions and reflect on how they are displayed by the uptight person, and how you may unintentionally and unconsciously also display some of these. In addition, remember that having some of these and/or displaying them infrequently is a reflection of undeveloped parts of self, and is not enough to be termed as self-absorbed. In order to meet that designation, the person should have numerous such behaviors and attitudes displayed frequently over time.

### Attention Seeking and Admiration Hungry

Attention seeking describes wanting and acting to bring others' attention to oneself. Example behaviors include:

- Acting out in inappropriate ways
- Becoming needy, sullen, or a martyr

- Talking loudly
- Telling stories and/or jokes instead of participating in conversations
- "Performing" or being "on stage"

Admiration hungry behaviors and attitudes include:

- Boasting and bragging
- Taking unearned credit
- Frequent self-nominations for honors and awards
- Acts to make the person appear as being helpful but that are really to garner appreciation
- Membership in numerous social and civic organizations to the extent that family and other intimate relationships are neglected
- Being a workaholic
- Inflation of personal achievements

Children and adolescents can enhance their self-esteem and feelings of self-adequacy when they receive adequate *attention and admiration*, and some of their behavior targets these needs. However, the same behaviors that are acceptable and expected for children and adolescents can signal undeveloped narcissism when exhibited by an adult.

**Lack of Empathy and Emptiness**

A lack of empathy can be identified by the following behaviors and attitudes: seems as if every conversation turns to his/her concerns; focus on content when others are speaking and ignores feelings; incomplete listening; ignoring emotions of others; can express the feeling word(s) but does not have the feeling; changes the topic when others are speaking. *A lack of empathy* has a significant negative effect on relationships. While it is not possible or feasible to be fully empathic with everyone all of the time, it is reasonable to expect adults who value a relationship to be empathic much of the time. The extremely uptight person has such a strong self-focus that he/she is not empathic with anyone, and others feel this lack of understanding for them and their concerns. A lack of empathy is illustrated when the uptight person does any of the following frequently, or almost all of the time:

- Changes the topic without first responding to what was said by the other person

- Responding only to the message's content, and ignoring or dismissing or diminishing the feeling part
- Interrupting others when they are speaking
- Not letting others finish what they are saying, "putting words in their mouths"
- Inferring others' motives, usually negative ones
- Appearing bored or uninterested when others are talking
- Telling someone that they should not feel as they are feeling

You probably can think of many more examples that illustrate a lack of empathy. It is difficult to describe emptiness as that is nothing. What is meant here is that the core of the person's self did not develop and there is a deep emptiness there. This nothingness is frightening and the person expends considerable effort to keep from experiencing it such as:

- Activities for activity's sake, and/or self-destructive acts
- The person is unable to form and maintain satisfying, meaningful, and enduring relationships
- Many failed relationships
- Lack of meaning and purpose for one's life

### Inappropriate Humor and Shallow Emotions

Examples for an inappropriate sense of humor include telling and laughing at ethnic, racial sexist, ageist jokes and stories; finding humor in others' discomfort, inadequacies, disabilities, and the like; or using sarcasm, put-downs, and the like where they can say that they were joking or teasing if the person objects.

Shallow emotions describe someone who does not experience or express a wide range or depth of emotions, Further, the emotions they do experience seem to be limited to mainly anger and fear; they do not understand gradations of feelings, such as the levels of contentment from pleasure to happiness to joy.

### Grandiosity and the Impoverished Ego

Grandiosity is an inflated perception of self. Children and infants are expected to have an inflated perception of self, where they are the center of the universe and others only exist to serve them. Adults are expected to have sufficient self development to not have this inflated perception of their importance and of the roles in their lives for others. Overcommitments for time and efforts; the assumption that others must always meet their needs, wishes, and demands; and an inability to recognize and accept one's personal limitations can be indicative of grandiosity in adults. In addition, this person can also display arrogance and contempt for others.

The flip side of the inflated self is the deflated self, or impoverished self. This is the "poor me, look how I suffer," helpless or even hopeless self. Feelings that one can never "get it right" or measure up to other's expectations, and a constant search for approval and liking can be indicators of the impoverished ego.

*Grandiosity* is what could be termed an inflated self and sense of one's self-importance, and an accompanying perception of others as being inferior. The flip side of grandiosity is an *impoverished ego*, and not only can both states exist in the same person, they can also change prominence in the presenting self rapidly. That is, the presenting self that you see when in an interaction, or when observing the person, can first show grandiosity, and then change to the impoverished ego as you talk with the person. To illustrate how rapidly this can occur, reflect on the following scenario.

*You are talking with someone who seems a little down, and you are being sympathetic to their problem. You make comments to let the person know that you care and understand. However, their response to your comments suggests or says that you have it wrong; they have no reason for concern as they are on top of their problem. This may even be said with the unspoken message that you are wrong or out of line in what you said.*

You are left feeling that you were in error with your response. Most likely, you were correct in your initial reading of the situation which led to you making the response that you did. But, in those few seconds, the impoverished ego state changed places with the grandiose state, and it was the grandiose state that suggested you were in error. Since that person is not aware of what he/she is doing, that only adds to the confusion. He/she is wondering why you responded as you did, and you are left wondering how you could misunderstand so badly.

What are some behaviors that can be suggestive of grandiosity?

• Agreeing to assume responsibility for numerous tasks that lead to overcommitment, that is trying to do too much

- Advice-giving where the assumption is that you know what others should or ought to do
- Arrogant and contemptuous acts and demeanor
- Taking over and running things even when someone else is in charge
- Making decisions that involve others without consultation
- Displays of impatience when having to wait, when others don't do as is wanted, and/or insisting that things be done in a particular way
- Making pronouncements, demands, and the like, with the expectation that these will be accepted and acted on without question or dissent

The impoverished self is seen in the following behaviors:

- Acting helpless
- Expressing hopelessness as a means to gain sympathy
- Complaints about unfairness, mistreatment, and so on, for almost everything and/or when objective reality indicates otherwise
- Self-depreciating comments, especially those that are intended to have the other person disagree with these
- Making comments about how others are receiving preferential treatment, especially about their unsuitability for receiving preference
- Reacting as if everything said or done is directed at you as a personal put-down, i.e. taking things personally
- Whining, carping, complaining, kvetching

**Exploitation and Extensions of Self**
The self-absorbed person can exploit others by exhibiting the following behaviors and attitudes:

- Using others to get one's personal needs, wishes, and desires met with no thought given to the impact on the other person
- Expecting and demanding favors with no reciprocity
- Taking advantage of others' good natures, ignorance, or gullibility
- Manipulating others to do things they do not want to do or that are not in their best interests in order to gain an advantage, or to get something from them

Extensions of self refer to having poor psychological boundaries, where others are perceived as extensions of oneself and not as separate and distinct individuals. Others, as extensions of self, can and should be controlled. Examples of behavior that can signal this perception of self and of others are as follows:

- Giving orders and expecting that these will be promptly obeyed, unless this is a function of a position such as in the military
- Expecting others to read your mind and provide what is wanted or needed without having to verbalize it
- Demands that others accept your values without questions
- Taking over others' territory, personal space, and/or possessions

### Entitlement and Envy

An entitlement attitude conveys the expectation that whatever the person desires will be forthcoming from others because of their being more deserving and special, that rewards and the like will be forthcoming without their having to put forth the effort to earn these. The person demands and expects deference and preferential treatment from others.

Envious people have a perception that others did not earn or deserve what they get or have, and that they are more deserving and meritorious than are other people. They also tend to resent the good things that happen for others, are deeply desiring what others have that they do not, and denigrate others to illustrate their unworthiness and inferiority.

Although external behavior can be observed, it is also suggestive of the person's internal landscape. Chapter 3 addresses the thoughts, feelings, reactions, and past experiences that form the uptight person's inner self.

# 3

# A Bleak Landscape: The Uptight Person's Internal Life

This chapter provides some information that suggests clues about why the uptight person acts as he/she does, especially when those acts are negative and destructive for others and for their relationships. In addition, this material can help you understand why your efforts thus far to understand and cope did not fully succeed, and can provide clues for developing more effective ways to protect yourself and to cope if you have to maintain the relationship. That is, you cannot leave the job, or you have to stay in the intimate relationship, and/or you want or have to maintain the relationship with your parent(s).

Let's begin with a short visualization of a possible internal landscape for an uptight person. I am terming it a landscape so that the identification of abstract concepts can be illustrated with known objects.

## Exercise 3.1
### Internal Landscape

*Directions:*

1. Find a place to complete the exercise where you will not be disturbed. Writing your responses to later questions is optional. If you choose to write, be sure to have some paper and a pen or pencil at hand.
2. Read through the following scenario and answer items 3 and 4.
   *Assume you are a space explorer who lands on an unknown planet. You are alone, and your spaceship takes care of all your needs. The spaceship devices have given you sufficient information so that you know the air*

*can be breathed without using your spacesuit's helmet, there does not appear to be dangerous beings or animals where you landed; and it is safe for you to go outside and walk around. Visualize any landscape you wish, what the sky and ground look like, what appear to be plants or other objects such as rocks, and/or if there is a body of liquid similar to water.*

*You leave the safety of the spaceship and step onto the ground, carrying your helmet and other devices. What you see, hear, and have sensations of are the following. All of this happens at the same time.*

- *You hear numerous voices that you cannot understand, but they are making noises that are uncomfortable, unsettling, and appear to you as menacing.*
- *The ground beneath your feet is constantly shifting so that you cannot maintain your balance.*
- *You look around, and the objects you see appear to you as angry, hostile, and vengeful faces, and you realize that these are the sources of the voices. These are all around you on every side.*
- *As you start to walk, the landscape changes abruptly, but the voices don't cease, and the ground still shifts.*
- *You decide to return to the spaceship, but you cannot see it even though you just left it and only took a few steps. Your devices don't work, and the landscape once again changes.*

3. What feelings do you have as you visualize yourself on this planet? You probably can identify with fear, dread, anxiety, and maybe even panic. Nothing seems fixed, safe, or secure, and is constantly in a state of flux and chaos. The loss of connection with the spaceship can be especially acute as that was your haven and protection.

4. Now, imagine that these images and feelings lurk just below the surface of your awareness, and in your unconscious. They stand ready to emerge in a nanosecond, or bubble up unconsciously or unexpectedly, and influence your conscious thoughts, behaviors, reactions, feelings, and so on without your awareness. They are both suppressed and repressed, but are also constant companions. The result could be that, although you try to control the fear, dread, and so on, and also try to control the external environment so that these internal states are not triggered, you have little or no success at controlling either. This is what contributes to your remaining intense and anxious and self-absorbed in order to protect your self.

If you can put yourself in this scenario enough to feel some of these feelings, you can start to understand some of the implications for having such an internal landscape, and how that influences the person. The remainder of this chapter will focus on the inner life of the uptight person. You may also find that some parts of it fit you, and that you are unconsciously acting on the parts of your inner life that are a result of an interaction of your personality, your past experiences, and your level of self development. As you recognize that you can identify with some parts of the uptight person's inner life, you will gain more understanding about that person, and even begin to better understand how you differ from the person. This understanding can then allow you to moderate your responses so that you can interact with him/her with fewer, or none, of the resulting negative feelings that are difficult for you to relinquish, and to create strategies to help you cope better. In this chapter, you'll be asked to use your imagination, your understanding of your self, and your past experiences as part of the process for a deeper awareness and understanding of the uptight person in your life. These understandings can lead you to more creative ways of coping.

## INNER LIFE COMPONENTS

Following is a list of some parts of the inner life of the uptight person with brief descriptions. These are the foundation for what follows in this chapter.

- Chaos—Nothing is constant, reliable, or trustworthy; everything is subject to change at any moment; the person feels that he/she has few resources to cope effectively with changes or with what emerges.
- Fears—There are acute fears of destruction and/or abandonment, the person feels helpless to care for the self and cannot depend on others.
- Hostile and Attacking External World—The self is constantly under attack, and eternal vigilance is required to remain safe.
- A Siege Response—All resources are mobilized and used to protect the self; few if any resources can be available to connect in meaningful ways to others.
- Hypersensitivity—A siege response produces hypersensitivity to perceived danger from the external world; the person is unable to

rationally and reasonably evaluate the level and extent of danger and thus, takes no chances.

- Neither Centered Nor Grounded—The person feels at the mercy of unknown and uncontrollable internal and external forces, and is unable to feel that the self is secure; can be empty at the core of the self.
- Envious and Jealous—Thinks and feels that others have what he/she desires and longs for, but these others are not worthy or deserving. Fears loss of relationships, the resulting feelings of isolation and/or alienation, and of being inadequate to care for self.
- "Sweats the Small Stuff"—Everything and everyone poses a danger to the self which then leads to an overconcern about trivia, to seeing danger where none exists, exaggeration of unimportant concerns and events, and so on.
- Accumulates Small Stuff—The small stuff accumulates and expands to become vitally important. This is the material for grudges, continued and continual envy and resentment, feelings of unfair treatment and of being shortchanged in many ways, and of constantly feeling betrayed and disappointed.
- Tends to Fragment More under Stress—A strong cohesive self can buffer the negative effects from both internal and external forces, and allow the person to cope effectively. An uptight person lacks this cohesion and tends to fragment under stress, which is almost always present for him/her. In order to try and keep the self from flying apart even more, the person can adopt strategies such as shutting down his/her emotions, bullying others, and/or being easily frustrated.

Each component will be expanded and illustrated.

### Chaotic Inner World

The introductory visualization gave a stark illustration of what a chaotic inner world could be like and how it could be experienced. Nothing is settled, predictable, or reliable, and everything appears menacing and dangerous. True safety and security are only available at a remote source that cannot be accessed. Safety, for the moment, seems present but steps must be taken to protect the self from danger and to try to remain safe and secure. How can you keep your self safe and secure under these conditions? The constant fear of destruction is acute, and the fear of abandonment has been realized as the sources for safety and security (the spaceship and devices) are not available, not working, and/or cannot be accessed. In addition, there may be questions about self-efficacy, being good enough, and other self-doubts arising within you. You cannot count on support or caring from others, and the self may not be adequate for survival.

It's bad enough when you live in a dangerous external world where there are numerous forces against your well-being, or that may even be trying to destroy you. Think about what people face living in neighborhoods where there are active drug and other criminal activities, including gunfire and random drive-by shootings, and what it is like for those who live in combat zones. The external threats and dangers are real, and there is little that an individual can do to protect him/herself. However, there are things that can be done to provide protection, and people do survive. The chaos can be somewhat manageable, and there are pockets of sanctuary where safety and security can be found, if only for the moment. The chaotic inner life of the uptight person does not offer any respite, safety, sanctuary, or security at any time.

A chaotic inner life is not easily managed because of several factors:

- A centered, grounded, and cohesive self which can serve as a buffer for adversity was never developed.
- The external chaos in their lives was internalized as "normal," and is still perceived as such.
- Many internal experiences are unconscious, and thus unknown to the person.
- It can be difficult to describe, verbalize, or even cognitively explain what is being experienced.
- Self-needs are imperfectly understood.
- The primary purpose is survival of the self, and little or nothin else can be contemplated or explored.

Nothing is reliable or dependable or predictable within oneself, and this is projected unconsciously onto the external world whether or not it is that way. There can never be enough external reassurance, safety, predictability, and so on, that fulfills the internal need. The chaos within cannot be controlled, managed, or even understood by the person.

### Fears

All humans seem to have two basic fears that are present at birth, the fear of destruction and the fear of abandonment. These fears underlie many feelings and behaviors and are significantly influenced by early experiences, especially those encountered in the family of origin. Reflect on the following common and usual feelings, and rate your experiences with these.

**Exercise 3.2**

**Fears**

*Materials:* A sheet of paper, and a pen or pencil

*Directions:* Find a place to work where you will not be disturbed. Use the following scale to rate your experiencing:

5–Very frequently, always, or almost always
4–Frequently, most often
3–Occasionally, sometimes
2–Rarely, infrequently
1–Never, or almost never

Rate your experiencing for:

1. Shame, embarrassment, or humiliation                          5 4 3 2 1

2. Feeling inadequate, or not good enough                        5 4 3 2 1

3. Jealousy and/or uncertainty about the strength of a     5 4 3 2 1
   relationship

4. Envy of someone's achievements, success, and/or         5 4 3 2 1
   possessions

5. Wanting or desiring others' approval and                      5 4 3 2 1
   acceptance

6. Feeling more accomplished and the like than many       5 4 3 2 1
   others

7. Feeling that you are disadvantaged and/or less            5 4 3 2 1
   accomplished, less successful, and the like than are
   many others

8. Feeling like the "cards are stacked against you," and  5 4 3 2 1
   resenting your plight and/or others' success

9. Dreading others' disapproval or disappointment           5 4 3 2 1
   and working to prevent this

10. Doing things you don't want to do in order to              5 4 3 2 1
    please other(s)

Scoring: Add your ratings to derive a total score.

| | |
|---|---|
| 43–50 | Extremely fearful |
| 35–42 | Very fearful |
| 27–34 | Fearful |
| 19–26 | Somewhat fearful at times |
| 10–18 | Little or no fear |

The total ratings at each end, extremely and little or no fear, are those that may call for some attention by you. An extremely fearful person may find that he/she is acting in a self-destructive way because of his/her unconscious fears. The little or no fear total ratings can suggest a person who is very cut-off or alienated from others to the point where he/she does not have or maintain lasting, meaningful, or satisfying relationships.

Now that you know something about the extent of your fears, you can begin to understand how the uptight person can be acting out his/her fears. This person probably falls into the extreme or very fearful category, and is constantly acting to prevent destruction and abandonment.

The uptight person also is probably not aware that his/her actions are fueled by these fears, and is able to point out evidence of his/her competencies to support the contention that he/she doesn't have these fears. It could be helpful to remember that much about their fears are unconscious, that objective reality does not reach these fears to reassure or moderate them, and that the fears are very much illogical and irrational, but also have a logical and rational component, albeit a small one. These fears are deeply entrenched and largely unknown to the person.

## Hostile and Attacking External World

It's no secret that the world can pose physical and psychological dangers. But most people have learned how to assess the threats, to prevent some harm, and when to fight and when to flee. While you probably never get it right all of the time, you do get it right often enough to have confidence that you can recognize a threat, or take steps to reduce or eliminate the possibility of the threat, or to defend yourself if need be.

The most difficult threats to recognize, prevent, or defend against are those that attack your internal self, or that arouse unpleasant and sometimes uncontrollable emotions. For example, think of how you feel and react when a close friend, relative, or lover unexpectedly says something that appears to you to be blaming or critical about you. Many people react with hurt feelings, anger, shame, or other such negative feelings. Your self, or your perception of your self, feels assaulted and you react in some way. However, it is likely that you are not constantly feeling attacked, or on guard around everyone, just at those times when you do feel attacked or assaulted or are interacting with someone who constantly belittles, demeans, or in some way attacks your self. You don't always expect attacks and you are not always defensive against possible attacks. You can exercise some evaluation and judgment.

The uptight person stays in the expecting attack mode, and tends to see hostility and attacks where none exist, or where none were meant. Their self stays in an under-siege, readiness-for-attack position, and this can produce the following:

- Difficulty in allowing intimacy
- Mounting unexpected attacks on others as defenses or as prevention
- Vengeful about real or imagined slights, put-downs, and the like
- Being rigid and stubborn
- An inability to relax, as this would weaken their guardedness
- Perceiving others who disagree with them as enemies
- Acting wary and tentative toward others

If you want to know what this feels like, try expanding your feelings for the example in the preceding paragraph to be a hundred times greater than what you normally experience even under adverse situations. These expanded feelings are similar to what the uptight person feels all or almost all of the time. Their perception of the external world is that it is always poised to attack their self.

### The Siege Response

Perceptions of the external world as hostile, dangerous, and poised to attack the self produce a siege response. Nothing gets in or out, eternal vigilance is used to stay aware of the possibility of attacks, everything and everyone is a potential source of danger and, while there may be a longing and yearning for meaningful connections, the person cannot lower their defenses long enough for any relationships to be established because that might give the hostile attacking forces an opportunity to access the self. Think about the terror experienced when you contemplate the destruction of your self, and then think of what it is like to always be in a state where you can never let down your guard. This is part of what the uptight person experiences all or most of the time.

The siege response takes the following forms:

- Noticing when things are not in order and that arouses anxiety
- Becoming and staying extremely anxious and intense when faced with ambiguity and uncertainty
- Checking and re-checking excessively to prevent errors, mistakes, accidents, and so on
- Retaining and/or collecting things of no value or that are essentially useless because you think that they may be needed in the future
- Quick to take offense to protect the self
- Little or no empathy for or with others
- Suspicious, mistrusting, and skeptical about others and their motives; sees danger in everything and everyone and has to be constantly on guard
- Resists and fights even small changes

The siege response produces a person behind the walls of his/her own making, as the perceived dangers are sometimes fantasized. A difficulty is that sometimes the dangers are real, but the uptight person cannot realistically assess the threat and vary their responses.

### Hypersensitivity
The uptight person is overly reactive to both internal and external experiences. This person automatically assumes the direst reasons for his/her experiences because of their tendency to expect the worst. He/she inflates symptoms, concerns, and perceptions of danger; has an inability to adequately assess experiences and their danger potentials; needs to protect the self at all times from perceived threats; and has a deep sense of personal inadequacy. These states lead to the hypersensitivity to self and to others.

This doesn't mean that some symptoms, concerns, and so on, are not valid. It just means that there is an overreaction to whatever the person is experiencing, and that the reaction is to always assume catastrophic outcomes; their attempts to ward off their fears that they will be inadequate to deal with it leads to the hypersensitivity.

The automatic assumption that what others say and do is directed at destruction of the uptight person's self leads to the hypersensitivity, and to the actions taken to protect the self. These people seem to always think and feel that all critical and blaming comments are directed at and about them even when they were not; that they alone are responsible for others' discomfort or disappointment; and/or that they will be abandoned or destroyed because of their inadequacy in taking care of others so that others do not feel distress, discomfort, or disappointment. The unrealistic and irrational expectations that uptight people carry about themselves can be overwhelming. They ward off feelings of inadequacy by off-loading the negative feelings onto others, especially those who are nearby or who are in some sort of relationship with them, or anyone who is open and receptive to receiving the blame and criticism that the uptight person feels and wants to get rid of. They are less effective in doing this when others are closed or defended against incorporating the projected negative feelings. Fortifying your self to be less receptive could be a major accomplishment to resist these projections. Chapters 9 and 10 provide some guidance for building these strong and resilient psychological boundaries that aid in resisting incorporating others' projected feelings.

## Lacking Centeredness and Groundedness

When you have a strong and cohesive self you are centered and grounded almost all of the time. External events and momentary lapses in judgment can cause you to be temporarily adrift, but you quickly find and secure your core self and return to being centered and grounded. If this describes you, then you are one of the fortunate people who seldom lose their sense of self and go off course too far. I've been fortunate to know two such people who have a strong core self and seldom become adrift. But when this happens, they are able to return to being centered and grounded.

It's not hard to empathize with feeling off center and adrift as most everyone has experienced feeling this way at some point(s) in their lives: external events, such as the loss of a loved one, being rejected or betrayed by someone you trusted, failure of any kind, the effects of a recessive and/or depressed economy, and other such situations usually not under your control. There are also internal events, such as aging, illness, irrational and unrealistic thoughts and/or expectations that can never be achieved, a lack of personal growth and development such as undeveloped narcissism, and so on. When any of these are experienced, you can feel adrift, indecisive, lacking in clear direction, dissatisfaction with oneself and with others, and other such feelings that signal a lack of centeredness and groundedness. The uptight person stays in this state and, if there is also sufficient undeveloped narcissism, their core self is empty and there is no way for them to anchor their self.

Think about what it would be like to always feel adrift, to be at the mercy of external and internal forces that you did not understand, could not control, and that seem very dangerous and bent on the destruction of your self. Add to this constant self-doubts about your ability to cope and survive. When these are combined, they can produce someone who is not resilient, lacks hardiness, and has considerable concerns about his/her self-efficacy. These states, thoughts, and feelings can lead to many self-destructive acts, and acts destructive against and toward others. These people realize that something important is missing, but they don't know what that something is, nor do they have any clues about how to understand what is needed, or how to obtain it.

## Envy and Jealousy

Think of envy as resentment of what others have that you lack and want. You feel that you are more worthy than they are, and think it unfair that they seem to be favored or more fortunate than you. Think of jealousy as resenting others who appear to be attractive to someone you are in a relationship with, and feeling that attractiveness has the potential to supplant your position with the relationship person. You fear the loss of the relationship, or some diminution of the quality of that relationship. Envy and jealousy are similar in many ways, but you can envy strangers, such as celebrities, whereas you are jealous of someone you know and who is in a relationship with you, such as a sibling or a co-worker.

Almost everyone can experience some envy and jealousy on occasion, but these are not part of their everyday existence. Something, usually an event or comment, arouses these, but they don't linger. This is not the case with the uptight person. They continually experience envy and jealousy which are fueled by their fears of inadequacy, being fatally flawed, becoming abandoned and/or destroyed, and of their ability to control others. Their self-absorption puts them at the center of the universe where they perceive everyone else as being of lesser status, of little or no consequence, and existing to serve them, the uptight person. Thus, when this self-absorbed self-perception is shaken, and the fears emerge, they become and act illogically and irrationally. These fears of abandonment and/or destruction are acute, and they perceive their self as being in imminent danger of becoming overwhelmed. They remain convinced that they deserve what they want, and it is others' place to move aside and get out of their way. Many of their negative actions are unconsciously designed to get what is wanted and, in their perception, is deserved. Their actions can be some or all of the following:

- Comments and actions to undermine the credibility and/or accomplishments of the envied person, or the target of their jealousy
- Deliberate lies and misleading statements to and about the person
- Withholding information, resources, and so on, so that the other person is at a disadvantage
- Violating confidentiality or trust to gain an advantage
- Negative comments, sarcasm, and/or put-downs to devalue the other person, and/or his or her accomplishments
- Becoming more whiny, needy, and complaining
- Inflates his/her personal qualities and/or accomplishments, boasts and brags to show superiority

It's difficult to cope when you are the target of envy and/or jealousy as most of the other person's acts are hidden, indirect, and/or disguised. Even more troubling can be when the envious or jealous people hide their feelings so well that you have no clue as to what they are feeling, you continue to trust them, and may even make excuses for the behavior that hurts you.

### "Sweats the Small Stuff"

Uptight people are so intense, anxious, and self-absorbed that everything in their lives assumes enormous importance and is crucial for their existence. Nothing is small, trivial, or inconsequential, and everything is targeted to and about them. They cannot let go of anything, they inflate the significance of everything, and they obsess over the need to fully control everything, even the uncontrollable. They cannot and do not understand why others don't feel as they do and accept the importance of everything. They feel that if others were more like them, then the small stuff would be prevented, eliminated, or handled so that they would not have to experience distress. They do not understand how anyone can accept randomness, things not being under their control, and/or that something could be unimportant in the grand scheme of things, or not consequential to their lives.

Of course, there are individual differences in the perception of what is "small stuff." What is important to one person may not be important to another person. But what is meant here is that the uptight person has no "small stuff" in his/her life; it's all major, important, and critical. A similar situation is seen in many adolescents where everything is so important, dramatized, and deeply felt. If someone is so rash as to suggest otherwise, they are treated with scorn, derision, and dismissal for not understanding. The uptight person can react as do some adolescents, and the atmosphere becomes tense and uncomfortable. This is one of the reasons why other people comply with the uptight person's need to address the "small stuff," and do what is necessary to keep him/her pleased. Examples of compliance include the following:

- Letting the boss micromanage, and stifling your initiative and creativity
- Becoming a "yes" person, and agreeing with everything that person says
- Being inauthentic, such as providing insincere flattery, saying you agree when you do not, and the like
- Doing things exactly as the other person wishes or desires, for example, loading the dishwasher as they dictate
- Never suggesting alternatives or options to what the uptight person proposes
- Never asserting your needs, wishes, or desires
- Choosing your words carefully most of the time for fear of upsetting him/her

The bottom line is that many people have priorities for what they consider as important and critical. The uptight person does not have priorities when it relates to him/her.

## Small Stuff Accumulates

Many or even most people do not dwell on the "small stuff." They note it, and let go of it. This is not possible for uptight people; they neither forget it nor let go of it. They can even expand it so that it becomes even more inflated and serious. In addition, they accumulate small stuff and use this as evidence that they are right, or are being disadvantaged, or that they are suffering, and so on. They can see connections between acts where none exist, make inferences that are illogical and irrational, and perceive assaults against their self that are fantasies or, even if these are real, they do not present any significant danger. For example, just because someone makes a comment that could appear to suggest you are inadequate, that doesn't mean that you are inadequate even if the person who made the comment intended it as a slight. Uptight people blow almost everything out of proportion, and use real and fantasized past offenses as evidence of intent and fuel for their resentment. This state of affairs is mainly internal, can be unconscious, and they can seldom verbalize these thoughts and feelings. However, these are seen in some of their behaviors and attitudes, like the following:

- Holding on to grudges for minor offenses, and collecting grudges
- Bringing up past offenses when in an argument over present events or situations
- Charging some with "you always," or "you never"
- Overreacting to imagined offenses, or something trivial
- Insisting on perfection for almost everything, including things that are inconsequential
- Inflating even the smallest change in anything
- Reciting chapter and verse of every offense they've experienced; these incidents remain acutely painful to them, even when others forget because the incidents were minor and/or fleeting

Their tendencies to accumulate the "small stuff," and to use these items as blame, criticism, and support for their attacks on others make them very uncomfortable to be around, to have casual conversations with, or to confide in. You can stay edgy yourself when you are in their presence, be tentative and cautious in conversations and choose your words carefully, and resist bringing up any topic that could provide a bridge to their real or imagined grievances.

### Fragments under Stress

Stress can be upsetting for almost everyone, and many people do not handle stress in constructive ways. Uptight people in particular can fragment under stress as they are not centered and grounded to begin with. Fragmenting under stress means here that the person has difficulty or cannot manage and contain their emotions, does not think clearly or logically, is unable to make reasonable and accurate assessments about the situation, is panicked and overcome by fear of possible destruction, and uses ineffective methods to maintain control of self and others. The less than cohesive self of the uptight person becomes even less cohesive, and the person can have an acute unconscious fear of their self flying apart. This possibility can be terrifying.

Added to this state is the constant perception of continuous danger from external forces and a need to stay vigilant and ready to defend the self. All of this can produce reactions like the following:

- Unexpected and vicious verbal assaults on others
- Bullying behavior to try and maintain control, and to feel less inadequate and helpless
- Shutting down of any emotions other than fear and/or anger; the anger could be used to disguise their fear
- Becoming sullen and unresponsive
- Making unfair and untrue accusations against others
- Becoming even more rigid and inflexible
- A noticeable lack of empathy and/or consideration for how others may feel
- Indifference to the impact his/her negative comments have on others
- Using stress as an excuse for behaving badly, but not offering a real apology
- Becoming lost and mired in his/her anger and/or fear and unable to easily get out of these feelings
- Directionless, cannot or does not ask for assistance, and seeming to go off in several directions at once
- Confusing to self and to others
- Exhibiting panic at the unexpected, surprises, and the need for changes
- Intensifies micromanaging, lack of collaboration, and ineffective and inefficient decision making
- Can become intensely concrete and even more narrow in scope and focus; and can have an increased need, on top of the already very high one, for predictability

To get some sense of what fragmentation could feel like, imagine being in a hot air balloon in a storm where your steering and navigational devices don't work. You are helpless under the assaults of the fierce wind, rain, and lighting, any of which could mean a crash and death. Imagine your fears and other feelings in this situation, and then try to sense what this is like when you are not involved in a concrete situation but sense the same uncontrollable forces and the same potential outcome. There are other illustrations that can be used to simulate what fragmentation of the self feels like, and I invite you to create your own illustration. Doing so could help you understand the uptight person's reactions when under stress, and also have an added benefit of better understanding your personal reactions to stress.

## SUMMARY

This chapter was an overview of the internal landscape for uptight people in order to help provide some understanding of what triggers and fuels their fears and other negative emotions, their attacking and aggressive behaviors, and their lack of awareness of the impact of their behaviors on others. The next five chapters extend this information in the discussion by categorizing them into types of uptight people: the Impoverished-self Hoarder, the Spartan Withholding, the Indulgent and Entitled, the Controlling and Manipulative, and the Revengeful Complainer. These types may not be discrete as they were developed for ease of discussion, and the uptight person in your life may have characteristics of more than one type.

# 4

# Anxious about Deprivation: The Impoverished-self Hoarder Type

Some uptight people appear to others as having low self-esteem (an impoverished self), while others can appear as having excessive self-esteem (grandiosity). Both the impoverished state and the grandiose state can exist in the same person; these can switch in a nanosecond when interacting with others, leading to confusion for the other person, and each can be disguised or hidden. This is what can make for confusion—the discrepancy between others' perceptions of them. Some people only perceive the impoverishment, and others only see the grandiose state. Since both states can easily exist and quickly switch within the same person, it makes it difficult at times to adequately respond to the uptight person. Add to this the uptight person's intensity and anxiety, and you are faced with an extremely difficult situation when you try to interact with him/her. In addition, you don't understand what is happening, and you have your own known and unconscious internal states to deal with at the same time. Let's try and sort through some of this to gain a better understanding that can lead to suggestions for coping strategies.

## DESCRIPTION OF THE HOARDER

True hoarders cannot throw anything away, even trash and broken objects that cannot be fixed. These people are not simply collectors who have overly achieved. Collectors focus on acquiring things that they find personally appealing, valuable, or that relate to them in some way, and these collections are organized. Hoarders save everything, or almost everything, and cannot let go of anything and little or none of this is organized. If asked about the "things" that they hold on to, excuses are made about potentially needing them some day, or that they are going to repair them, or they will make an insincere promise to get rid of them and not follow through. You may be able to get some idea of what hoarders keep that is of no value or sentiment by completing the following exercise.

**Exercise 4.1**

**My Stash of Trash**

*Materials*: Your desk drawers, or a kitchen drawer, or a shelf in your closet. You can use a clothes or linen closet also.

*Procedure*:

1. Choose one of the above and remove each item in it, one by one.
2. Examine each item and put it into one of three piles:
   a. Keep—Valuable, or will be used
   b. Trash—I should discard this
   c. Donate—Has utility, but I can donate this to a worthy person or agency (Salvation Army, Goodwill Industries, or a nonprofit thrift shop)
3. Examine the keep pile and re-check to make sure an item does not belong in the other two piles.
4. Step back and examine the three piles:
   a. Which is largest?
   b. What has been kept beyond its utility value that is in the trash and donate piles?
   c. Did you remove anything from the trash or donate piles and move it back to the keep pile? Why?
5. Discard the trash pile, making sure that you are not throwing away someone else's possession. Once again, did you remove anything from this pile and return it to the keep pile?
6. Take a few minutes to reflect and identify the feelings you experienced as you examined each item, decided on its pile placement, and when you changed your mind and returned an item to the keep pile.

7. Try and follow through with the discarding and give away piles. Note your feelings as you do, or if you change your mind. Return the keep pile to the drawer, closet, or wherever it was.

You may not be in the same category as a hoarder, but it is the rare person who is not holding on to things that should be discarded or given away. As I write this, I am in the process of moving my office, and have an opportunity to repeatedly complete the exercise. My current office is very small, but I'm surprised and amazed at what I've held on to that should be discarded or given away in spite of my efforts to reduce these at the end of every semester.

The Impoverished-self Hoarder type emphasizes his/her impoverished self and does not limit the collections to things. While these collections may also be problematic, more troubling to relationships can be hoarding of the following:

- Other's comments and actions that are perceived by them as slights, put-downs, and devaluing of them in any way
- Imagined or fantasized hidden agendas, malicious motives, and/ or disguised assaults from and by others
- Deep disappointment and rage at others who are close to them for their failure to protect them from experiencing shame, guilt, and inadequacy, and they keep these feelings forever
- Grudges for narcissistic injury; they can neither forgive, forget, or move beyond the injury
- Fear of failure so acute that they limit their opportunities to advance at work, to acquire additional education, and/or to form meaningful relationships
- May try to ease or suppress their feelings of inferiority by exaggerating personal characteristics they consider to be superior

These can be acutely painful to the uptight person, easily accessed, but never moderated or eliminated. Let's examine each in more detail.

## HYPERSENSITIVE TO COMMENTS

The Impoverished-self Hoarder type take almost every comment made by anyone as directed personally toward them, even the most neutral ones. It is difficult to fathom the conscious and unconscious associations they can make that allow them to perceive these comments as criticizing, blaming, and/or devaluing. There are variations among these uptight people in the degree to which they are hypersensitive, but they all do tend to take things personally, and this tendency can make interactions with them difficult.

Many times, they are able to hide this hypersensitivity, but later conversations, their off-hand comments, and so on, will reveal their true perceptions—that those actions or comments were directed at them and were negative. At other times, they can be more present-centered and make comments that let the other person(s) in the interaction know that they perceived what was said as personally directed at them. In this case, what generally happens is that the other person(s) then spends time denying, protesting, and/or reassuring the uptight person. The real topic or focus becomes lost, and the uptight person becomes the focus. Also, it is just about impossible to change their minds about the intent and perceived personal nature of the initial comment. They may back away, say that they understand that no negativity was meant, and so on, but they haven't really changed their minds. You can count on this surfacing in future comments, interactions, and/or conversations in some form.

This type collects and hoards these as validation of their impoverished self. It's almost like they are saying, "See, I knew I was flawed, and you recognize it, too." Just think about what it would be like to get constant validation of your flaws, inadequacies, imperfections, and the like, and to constantly be in pain at the very thought of these. Or, what it is like to constantly be on the lookout for this kind of validation. It seems to me that their alertness and hypersensitivity contribute to the edginess of uptight people, especially this type. They are both fearing this negative validation, almost always searching for it, and perceive it in paractically everything others say.

*What to Do.* Most of the recommended strategies are what not to do to manage the Impoverished-self Hoarder's hypersensitivity. These are presented because they are common responses when the other person feels that what you said was directed at him/her, and that the comment was blaming and/or shaming. These usual responses are generally received positively by uptight people and, in some cases, can worsen the situation. The actions to avoid are listed first.

- Don't protest their perspective and tell them that it is wrong. They will not believe you, and it will harden their position.

- Don't suggest that they are overreacting or are hypersensitive. This can add fuel to their anger.
- Don't try to compensate with a compliment. They cannot believe you, or accept that you mean what you say.
- Don't overexplain. Doing so just confirms their perspective that you were blaming them, or trying to shame them, and are now being defensive.
- Don't try to joke or shame them out of their perspective. They will then feel that you don't understand, and/or are deliberately trying to hurt them.
- Don't become defensive and/or attack them. That is validating and confirming what they perceive as your evil intent for them.
- Do try to give a quiet non-defensive response, such as saying that you meant something different, then saying what that something was.
- If your word choice was poor, say so and correct it.
- Try to remember their hypersensitivity and choose your words accordingly when interacting with them.

## IMAGINED/FANTASIZED HIDDEN AGENDAS

Hidden agendas are common for most everyone, can be conscious or unconscious, affect what the person does or says, and are generally considered as being self-serving for that person. People who have conscious hidden agendas are not genuine at that moment or in the current interaction, and can be trying to manipulate others for their personal advantage or to put the other person(s) at a disadvantage. While hidden agendas may be common, many people do not interact or operate based on these all of the time. Hidden agendas may be used for special occasions when the person feels that being upfront and genuine is not in his/her best interests. However, there are people who almost always have hidden agendas, and use these to manipulate others.

It's difficult to describe unconscious hidden agendas, but they also affect an individual's thoughts, feelings, and actions, and do so unbeknownst to that person. You are not aware of your unconscious hidden agendas, and may never know how these are affecting you. Because this is a complicated and complex topic that needs more time and space to discuss properly, we'll just accept that there are unconscious hidden agendas, and limit our focus to conscious ones.

The Impoverished-self Hoarder type can perceive everyone as having hidden agendas that are directed at them, are negative, and are designed to destroy them. They see danger at every turn and from everyone, and can fantasize hidden agendas where none exist. Nothing others say or do is taken at face value, and is openly or covertly questioned as to the hidden meaning and/or intent. While some uptight people are always on guard for feared assaults on the self, this type is almost always so.

The other side of this stance is that these uptight people do have conscious hidden agendas when interacting with others, and cannot imagine that others are different and do not also have these. Many uptight people do want to manipulate others to maintain their own safety; they don't understand others as being separate and distinct individuals not under their control, and they assume that all others feel and think as they do. This perspective is a part of their undeveloped narcissism where they have not developed sufficient psychological boundary definition between their self and others. Their assumptions are that others are seeking to destroy them, and that they have to take steps to prevent this from happening. This is one reason why they see real and fantasized hidden agendas in others, and are unable to fully trust anyone.

*What to Do.* The suggested strategies are based on the futility of expecting the uptight person to change, even if you are in an intimate relationship with him/her. His/her desire to preserve the relationship may help moderate the behavior somewhat, but will not be sufficient to eliminate it. Expect that he/she still looks for hidden agendas even when nothing is openly expressed.

- Don't be defensive when challenged about having a hidden agenda, or when he/she infers that you have one.
- Become more aware of your conscious and possible unconscious hidden agendas.
- Accept that you will never be fully trusted by the uptight person. Since this is more about him/her than it is about your trustworthiness, try to not be resentful or hurt.
- Be authentic and genuine in your actions, expressions of feelings, and in other verbalizations.
- Refrain from chastising or challenging him/her about the mistrust.
- Become more aware of when you may be trying to manipulate him/her, and other people, since when you try to manipulate others, he/she expects that you will also try to manipulate him/her.

## UNFAIR TREATMENT

It is the unusual person who has not felt treated unfairly at some point in life, and most of us can identify and sympathize with how this can arouse resentment and rage. There is an accompanying feeling of impotence or helplessness to prevent the unfairness, or to remedy it and thus restore fairness. No matter that fairness may be an illusion, or dependent on personal perspective, we all know what fair treatment is for us, and we want and expect it. The difference for some self-absorbed uptight people is that they do not ever relinquish the aroused resentment and rage; they carry these with them throughout their lives, and every time they recall the incident(s), that rage and resentment are still as fresh and hurtful as they were when the incident happened. They do not forget, forgive, or move on. Some may cognitively be able to excuse the act(s), and/or rationalize them, but still carry the underlying feelings which can be evident when they talk about the incident. When they do, they can usually recall every detail. They tend to collect and hoard every incident where they felt unfairly treated, and stay stuck in those feelings.

There can be a lot of shame associated with being unfairly treated as those acts send messages of inadequacy, not being good enough for fair treatment, inferiority to others, and of the possibility of being abandoned and destroyed for perceived fatal flaws. It doesn't matter if the unfair treatment is significant, trivial, unimportant, unintentional, real, or fantasized, as their feelings about one's self and about others get triggered regardless. When the act is trivial or unimportant, most people can let go of it and move on. They can realistically assess the situation, take needed actions, and distance themselves enough to not let it continue to exert negative effects on them. Uptight people cannot use these inner resources, and so they continue to hold on to the negative feelings. They are convinced that they are in the right, and that they should feel as they do.

*What to Do.* You have to accept that nothing you do or say will get this type of uptight person unstuck. This is difficult to accept as you probably have recovered and moved on from many of your own unfair treatment incidents. You can better understand the uptight person's perspective if you also have one or more past incidents of unfair treatment in your life that you still carry with you, and they still can arouse intense feelings when you recall them. You probably have others where you have distanced yourself and moved on, but you may also have a few that are not yet resolved and relinquished. Try the following exercise for a better understanding of the Impoverished-self Hoarder type person(s) in your life.

**Exercise 4.2**

**It's Not Fair**

*Materials*: Two sheets of unlined paper; a set of crayons, colored pencils, or felt markers; and a pen or pencil for writing

*Procedure*:

1. Find a place to complete the exercise that will be free from intrusions and distractions. There should be a suitable surface for drawing and writing.
2. Sit in silence and reflect on times and incidents from your childhood or adolescence where you felt treated unfairly, and may even feel this way today. Make a list of these, even those that may seem trivial.
3. Review your list and select one incident.
4. Close your eyes, and recall that incident in as much detail as possible.
5. When you are ready, open your eyes, and using another sheet of paper draw a picture that captures the essence of the incident and of the unfairness. The picture can be representational or abstract.
6. Look at the picture you drew and list the feelings you experienced as you recalled the incident, and as you drew. Give each feeling an intensity rating from 0 (little or no intensity) to 10 (significant intensity). Note any feelings that are rated 5 or greater.
7. Select another sheet of paper, and for each feeling rated 5 or greater write a statement that associates that feeling with a thought or feeling about your self. Some suggestions are as follows:

Jealousy—fear of being abandoned, loss of the relationship
Anger—helplessness, unable to protect oneself
Resentment—not good enough, inadequate, inferior
Hurt—the self was not protected, either by oneself or by others
Revenge—the self can feel adequate when the other person is hurt
   or destroyed
Hopeless—I never will be good enough

8. Now, rate the validity of the feeling(s) from 0–little or no validity or no evidence to confirm this, to 10–very true about me as I am today.
9. Review the feeling(s), associations, and validity ratings. Ask yourself if you can let go of those that are not valid, or that have little validity.

If you can put yourself back into the exercise in steps 2–6, you can better understand how an uptight person feels all of the time or even more intensely than you, and how they have numerous perceived unfair treatment incidents that carry considerable intensity. This understanding is basic for the following suggestions for coping:

- Listen to their stories of unfair treatment, sympathize with their feelings, but do not try to empathize as you may become enmeshed or overwhelmed by their intensity.
- Make neutral comments. Don't take sides.
- Do not try to present a rational and/or logical perspective as the person perceives that as you telling him/her that he/she is wrong.
- Don't try to jolly them out of it. Humor will be perceived as your not taking them seriously.
- Don't try to distract them by focusing on their successes. This too can be perceived as your not understanding or taking them seriously.

## FAILURE TO PROTECT THEM

When an adult has considerable undeveloped narcissism, such as a Destructive Narcissistic Pattern (Brown, 1998), many of their thoughts, feelings, attitudes, and reactions are similar to those of infants, toddlers, children, and adolescents. Some examples for these include the following:

- Expecting others to defer to them, put their needs first almost always, and to know that they want or need and give this to them
- Others should anticipate their desires, wants, and needs without their having to verbalize these (mind reading)

- They can say whatever they want to others, e.g., blame and criticism, and others should accept this without protest; they may even pride themselves on "being honest," and feel that others would be better off if they too could be "honest"
- Others exist to serve them and should be diligent in doing so
- They are entitled to have what they want, when they want it, and others should promptly provide what is wanted

These, and other such thoughts, feelings, attitudes, and reactions may be unconscious on their part, but can still be troubling to others who are in relationships with them. This can be especially acute when accompanied with the intensity and anxiety seen in uptight people.

The developmental delay in growth of the self and, as part of that growth, the recognition of the separateness and distinctiveness of self and of others, can help you understand why the uptight person can have an unrealistic expectation that you and others are supposed to protect them from having to experience shame, guilt, and/or assaults from others. While some of their unrealistic expectations are a carry-over from their parental relationships, these are now being projected or transferred to their close adult relationships. Their deep disappointment and rage at what they perceive as your failure to keep them from experiencing these distressing feelings, and/or to prevent others from arousing these feelings within them, can stem from both their undeveloped self and from their early family of origin relationships. They can have an unconscious and unrealistic expectation for those close to them that they should not have to experience these feelings, and their reactions are blame, criticism, rage, and disappointment toward others. Others close to them may hear something like, "You are making me feel (a particular feeling)." But that is unfair as others do not make you have particular feelings, you cause these yourself. Some uptight people can have tantrums, go into tirades against the person close to them at the time, withdraw and sulk, and have other such negative reactions. They are angry and disappointed that you failed to protect them, regardless of how irrational that expectation may be.

*What To Do.* The following suggestions may be helpful:

- Recognize the limits of your responsibility for others' feelings.
- Accept that their feelings are theirs alone, and that you are not responsible for these being triggered, aroused, or experienced.

- Don't apologize or try to explain, as you probably don't know what you did or failed to do to warrant an apology or explanation.
- Don't accept emotional abuse, such as tantrums or tirades.
- Set clear, firm boundaries for what you can accept as your responsibility.
- Don't try to sweet-talk or cajole them out of a withdrawal or sulk.
- Acknowledge that their feeling, such as shame, can be difficult to experience or to deal with.

## GRUDGES FOR NARCISSISTIC INJURY

Narcissistic injuries are deep and painful. The self is shamed, perceived as inferior and inadequate, and there can be hopelessness, helplessness, and despair accompanying the other feelings. However, the self may employ a range of defenses to prevent these from being consciously experienced, but they are still present on an unconscious level, and are the basis for rage, resentment, and grudges. The person was injured, and when that injury does not heal, the initial injury can be re-injured numerous times, causing even more pain and making the initial injury even deeper. It becomes even more difficult for the injured person to forgive additional injuries and to allow healing. Thus, grudges can be born.

Many initial narcissistic injuries occur in childhood, and those that happen in early development are stored in memory in a form that cannot be retrieved in thoughts and language, and can even be deeply repressed. However, the injury remains, and subsequent narcissistic injuries build on top of the initial one. New injuries are not necessarily from the same kind of incidents as what caused the initial injury, but the new incidents produce the same kind of feelings about the self as did the initial incident.

Now, let's fast forward to the Impoverished-self Hoarder uptight adult who may have suffered an early narcissistic injury that is repressed, has encountered other such injuries that exacerbate the initial one so that healing cannot occur, and now in the present, has been reinjured once again. It becomes more understandable that grudges would be formed and maintained, not so much because of the current injury, but because of the accumulation of narcissistic injuries from others throughout the person's life that are combined and assigned to the current offender. Yes, that person did offend and institute a narcissistic injury, the actual offense may have been unintentional, trivial, or not personally directed at the uptight person, but even if apologies are extended, the uptight person cannot let go or move beyond the hurt.

This is a rather brief explanation of the complexity for grudges and narcissistic injury. What cannot be described very well are the acts that cause such injuries early in life. The person himself/herself lacks the words to describe the feelings and acts because many of these may have occurred in the pre-verbal era of their lives. Other injuries were encountered as the unrealistic demands of the developing infant and/or child, such as any delay in getting their hunger needs met. These can now be understood as irrational by the adult, but still carry the unconscious and deep injury that is not understood by him/her. Regardless of the unrealistic reaction and irrationality, the accumulation of injuries over a lifetime can be the basis for current grudges.

Grudges persist because of past narcissistic injuries, fears that the offending person will injure or destroy him/her, and reservations about one's personal effectiveness, adequacy, and worthiness. Grudges are a way to remind the person to be alert and on guard because of ever present dangers.

*What to Do.* If you are in a close relationship with an Impoverished-self Hoarder uptight person who carries grudges, you have probably heard about these offenses frequently and in detail. If the relationship is not close, such as a work related one, you may know of these grudges, but not in detail. However these emerge, frequently, infrequently, or as inferences, the following suggestions can provide guidelines for coping:

- Accept that nothing you do or say will resolve the grudge or cause the uptight person to be more rational and reasonable.
- Don't take sides. Listen and make neutral responses. Validate their feelings, but not the rationale for them.
- Don't say or do anything that hints that they are unreasonable in their perspective, should not feel as they do, or that they are being irrational. This could produce rage at you.

## FEAR OF FAILURE

Failure is not pleasant to contemplate or to encounter. It confronts us with evidence that we were not competent, adequate, or able. That can be difficult to accept, and makes it hard to continue feeling good about our self. Most of us meet with minor and major failures throughout our lives, and have developed compensating mechanisms to help us cope and to not be devastated by failure all of the time. We may even have learned to distinguish between trivial and major failures, and be able to let the trivial ones go, to make changes and corrections to prevent occurrences of new ones and reoccurrences of old ones, to not obsess and continually berate ourselves for not being perfect, and to work to build our hardiness and resilience. These are positive coping mechanisms that allow us to handle failure without becoming destroyed by it. We can recognize that all failures are not due to our inadequacies, and that some are out of our control and affected by other forces outside of us, such as policies and practices, economic forces, the political climate at every level, and even the weather. There are many such forces which affect us; we cannot control them, but they can contribute to our personal failures.

The Impoverished-self Hoarder type of uptight person takes all failures personally, even when they can cognitively recognize that there are outside forces that can contribute to or cause failure. Their levels of self-absorption—especially their grandiosity, arrogance, and entitlement attitudes—play a major role in their perceptions of failure as being solely under their control, and as making statements about their self as being inadequate, incompetent, and/or ineffective. Since everyone usually meets some sort of failure throughout life, it is not difficult to understand how uptight people's early failures could lead them to taking all failure as personal, and as making statements about them and their flaws. This can lead to them becoming fearful enough to exhibit the following:

- Almost always resists the new and unknown, and insists on sticking to what is known
- Refuses to take even minor risks
- May not work to achieve to capacity
- Resists competition
- Avoids everything that is ambiguous and uncertain
- Must have everything spelled out in detail
- Does not adapt well to changes, even when these are needed and/or unavoidable

*What To Do.* This fear of failure is deep, pervasive, and was developed over time, which means that it would be extremely difficult to overcome, moderate, or eliminate. With this caveat, the following suggestions are presented:

- Do not push them to take risks, as logic and encouragement are not sufficient to overcome the fear.
- Present them with as much detail as is possible and reasonable when making changes, or when they are facing ambiguous situations.
- When changes are necessary, plan and manage these, such as instituting them slowly and over time. Try to avoid abrupt changes.
- Be sensitive to how overwhelming the fear of failure is for them.
- Don't challenge them to competition.

## SUPPRESSION OF FEELINGS OF INFERIORITY

The impoverished self contributes to the perception of self as inferior and/or inadequate, but this is very shaming for the person, and so he/she takes action to prevent others from seeing this unworthy self. The fear is that to be seen by others leads to destruction and/or abandonment. In either case, the person does not survive.

Actions to try and hide a self that is self-perceived as impoverished and inferior can include the following:

- Exaggeration of perceived unfair treatment and so on, to explain lack of achievement, performance, and the like
- Continual recitation of real or imagined mistreatment by others that produced grievances, grudges, and so on
- Needing more and more detail in order to do almost everything
- Seeking reassurance of competency both directly and indirectly
- Collecting unneeded information and facts as a way to delay beginning anything
- Refusal to engage in discussions where others disagree with him/her
- Taking a stand and refusing to change, even in the face of new information
- Saying and doing things that emphasize their disappointment when not complimented enough, but will deny this if challenged
- Becoming very grandiose, arrogant, and contemptuous of others as not being as competent, skilled, moral, and so on, as he/she is, and/or of not trying hard enough

You probably can identify many more acts that signal a cover-up of an impoverished self. If you are in a relationship with such a person, it is helpful for you to understand that this self-perception is longstanding, a significant part of that person, and may not be fully known by him/her. Coping means awareness and acceptance of your limitations to moderate these acts and attitudes.

*What to Do.* Even though you may want to help the person to have greater and/or more realistic self-esteem, there is very little you can do, as much of this desired development has to come from within that person, and he/she has to make that decision to effect changes. Further, this person most likely sees no need for changes, is unaware of the possibility of any other way of being, and may even be convinced that his/her way is the right way and that others should be more like him/her. This attitude may be difficult for you to accept, but you will feel less frustrated and futile when you do recognize these limitations. Following are a few suggestions:

- Listen to their exaggerations and grievances, but do not try to challenge or explain these away. Make neutral responses, and try to understand their perspective without necessarily agreeing with it.
- Accept that you can never provide enough reassurance. When you do try to reassure and encourage, do so without becoming frustrated at its ineffectiveness, and at the endless need for this.
- Don't try to insert reason and/or logic, as this can suggest to them that you think that they are wrong to feel as they do.
- Don't abruptly change the topic. Doing so could convey to them your disinterest and does indicate some discomfort. If you think a topic change would be helpful to reduce some of their emotional intensity, first give a response that reflects what they said to let them know that you heard them. After which, you can say that you understand the importance to them, but you need to change the topic. At this point you should have something important to begin the discussion, such as a question or observation about something of importance.

# 5

# Depriving Self and Others: The Austere Withholding Type

The Austere Withholding type is characterized by a miserly attitude toward money in particular, which contributes to an austere lifestyle and withholding of physical, emotional, and relational resources. This attitude toward money is also projected and acted out in other parts of these people's lives. They learned and internalized early on that survival was possible and enhanced only when money or other resources were available, and they are always in a need-for-survival mode. They cannot let go of what they consider as essential for survival, and what must be collected and retained to be available at any moment.

Being a miser goes way beyond frugality, although the miser can characterize him/herself as frugal. Living within one's means, not carrying unneeded debt, understanding the difference between essential and non-essential spending, and the like, are frugality. In addition, frugal people do not deny themselves some pleasures, assuming that whatever it is falls within their spending guidelines. They can derive pleasure from their austere lifestyle, but austerity does not mean absence of all pleasure, or actual distress at the need to spend for essentials. Misers can feel distress at the need to spend for everything, deny themselves necessities in other to save money, withhold necessities from those who depend on them to obtain these, and are suspicious and disapproving of pleasure that requires any expenditure. This suspicion and disapproval are not limited to those things that cost money, they can be extended to activities. Holding on to what they have is extremely important to them, even at the expense of relationships, and the health and welfare of self and others.

A description of the Austere Withholding type would include three categories: what is withheld in interactions and relationships, indices of self-absorption, and general tendencies. Examples for each category follow:

## Withheld in Interactions and Relationships
This category includes the behaviors and attitudes usually associated with relational skills such as the following:

- Approval
- Appreciation
- Tolerance
- Respect for differences
- Trust
- Encouragement and support

*Approval* is withheld as little that others do is satisfactory, or meets their standards. Efforts from others are perceived as less than adequate, and uptight people, not just this type, can feel that it is deceiving to give approval for less than perfection; and the Austere Withholding type feel even more strongly about this. In some ways, they are as hard on themselves as they are on others with their unrealistic expectations for perfection that can never be achieved. They can be quick to see and point out errors, mistakes, imperfections, and the like, but are extremely slow to voice approval of others, or for almost anything.

You may long to hear the words that signal their approval, and work very hard trying to achieve this without any success. You can even wonder why they are unwilling to see and understand how much their approval means to you. It's not so much that they are unwilling as it is that they are unable to empathize and provide you with the approval you seek and probably merit. Don't forget that lack of empathy is one characteristic of the self-absorbed. If you can accept that they are unable to empathize, then you will be much less upset when approval is withheld. Challenging them about their lack of empathy, or unwillingness to give approval, is unlikely to produce any changes, and is likely to be turned back on you as an indication of your lack of standards and other inadequacies.

It can be disconcerting to frequently be confronted with your lapses, mistakes, and so on, and to not to have your efforts, achievements, and other positive attributes recognized with some acknowledgment and approval. You may find it helpful to reflect on your need for approval from the uptight person in your life who is this type, and begin to tell yourself that you are looking for something that is unlikely to be forthcoming, and to find other sources for the approval you're seeking.

*Appreciation*, like approval, can also be withheld because uptight people do not appreciate anything that doesn't exactly meet their needs, perceptions, and desires. Since they may not be aware of what these are, and/or not communicate them to others, it is an impossible situation. In addition, if someone were to point out that it would be gracious of them to show some appreciation, they would then be put on the defensive and resent being told that they were inadequate in their response, or that they have to appreciate less than perfection. Yes, they may show some civility and courtesy at times, or when pushed to do so, but they are less than genuine with this response, and can be very angry at having to show appreciation to you or to anyone else who does not precisely meet their conscious and unconscious needs.

Another aspect of the Austere Withholding type can be their lack of appreciation of other's positive qualities and attributes. They tend to minimize or overlook these, and define others in terms of their more negative attributes and qualities. Doing so allows them to feel superior, to consider others as inferior, and to be contemptuous of others' imperfections and flaws. While there certainly are some qualities and attributes that are negative—such as abuse of any kind, meanness, and manipulation of others for personal gain—that is not what is meant here. Examples of personal qualities and attributes that some perceive as negative, so as to allow their feelings of superiority and contempt for the person possessing these, can include the following:

- Racial/ethnic differences
- Gender
- Poverty status
- Family background
- Obesity
- Addiction
- Educational level

These people can fail to see the real person who has these qualities and attributes as having both strengths and flaws, and focus only on their perceived negative attributes They have real difficulty seeing others' positive attributes when others are different from them.

*Tolerance* for differences and mistakes does not seem to be a part of uptight people's makeup. They tend to feel that others should be like them, and that differing from them makes the person unacceptable, is a sign of inferiority, and cannot be tolerated. The Austere Withholding type will tend to be firm and steadfast in their perceptions and convictions that they are in the right, and that others should strive to be, and become more, like they are. This perception and conviction are so deep and pervasive that nothing you do or say changes any part of them. As far as they are concerned, the subject is closed and needs no further discussion. They think that you and others should spend your time and energy becoming more like they are.

This lack of tolerance for differences is not necessarily discrimination for attributes such as race, gender, and social class, although some or all of these can also be present. The lack of tolerance can also extend to include the following:

• Differences in perception of a person or of a situation
• Perception of an issue, problem, or concern, as well as the solution for these
• Doing something your way instead of his/her way
• Not following his/her directions, orders, or demands, but still achieving good results
• Lack of sympathy for other's misfortune because if that person was more like the uptight person, the misfortune would not have occurred
• Understanding how someone could make mistakes, errors, and the like

Since almost everyone makes mistakes, encounters misfortune or adversity due to errors of judgment, has different understandings of issues, problems, and concerns, perceives situations and people from their personal background and personality, and has their own way of doing things, uptight people have numerous examples of how they must be right and how others are constantly wrong and inferior.

*Respect for differences* is not a part of the Austere Withholding type's mind set, as noted in the previous section. A noticeable lack of respect for differences can be exhibited by many uptight people. Some indices of a lack of respect are nonverbal, and others are verbal. The arrogant and contemptuous attitudes are both conscious and unconscious, hidden or disguised, or can be openly displayed. Because these attitudes emerge from their deeply held convictions about what is right and wrong, and what is good and bad, and the absolute certainty that their position is the only valid one, it can be impossible to make any headway on convincing uptight people to moderate, change, or eliminate any of their cherished beliefs about the value and worth of those who differ. The Austere Withholding type can be especially difficult in that they withhold from almost everyone, and this extends to withholding respect for differences.

Let's examine some indices of respect to understand how the lack of respect can be identified by the absence of these.

- Responding directly to what others say in a way that conveys that they were heard and understood **before** presenting a response of another opinion or perspective
- A conscious absence of derogatory, dismissive, and devaluing remarks and comments about others, their opinions, and/or their values
- Refraining from telling others what they should or ought to do, believe, and so on
- Accepting differences without agreeing or incorporating them

Responding directly, and first responding in a manner that conveys that you heard what the other person said and your understanding of what was meant, can indicate respect for whatever differences there may be. You can then continue and add your comments. Even when you disagree with the other person, using this procedure will minimize misunderstandings and increase the other person's willingness to listen to your perspective.

It is very helpful to a relationship to not make derogatory, dismissive, and/or devaluing remarks about the other person when you disagree. These sorts of remarks can be very hurtful, indicate a lack of respect, and convey arrogance and contempt. Just because someone differs, does not mean that the person is wrong.

Another form of arrogance, entitlement, and grandiosity is telling others what they should or ought to do. This conveys a lack of respect for the other person, and is indicative of a lack of respect for differences. Not only does using "should" and "ought" make it appear that you are superior and know what is best for someone else, it also conveys that you perceive the other person as inferior and not capable.

It is most helpful to be able to accept other's differences knowing that these do not threaten you, and that you do not have to incorporate them or act on them; you can continue to have your own. You don't have to get the other person to incorporate your opinions, values, beliefs, and so on, nor do you have to incorporate theirs.

## TRUST

The Austere Withholding type finds it difficult or impossible to trust others, and tends to constantly and continually fear destruction. Further, their life experiences may have been such that mistrust is the first response. However, the uptight person can never fully trust anyone, and even when someone earns some measure of trust, this trust is not complete. It is always tentative, and subject to withdrawal at any moment. The uptight person is always on alert looking for any sign that the trust they gave is misplaced. Nothing you can do will produce full trust.

This lack of trust certainly contributes to others' uneasiness and frustration with the relationship, and in some cases, there can be numerous indices of a lack of trust, such as the following behaviors:

- Asking questions that seem to be an interrogation
- Demanding extensive details about almost everything
- Making comments that convey skepticism, but you cannot challenge these as their skepticism is not openly expressed
- Making remarks about yours and others' trustworthiness
- Micromanaging
- Checking up on you to see if you were accurate about things like where you were going, or what you are doing
- Telling you how something must be done, and then checking to ensure that you complied or obeyed

These and other such acts can arouse indignation, resentment, hurt, anger, and other negative feelings in the recipient. This can be especially damaging to an intimate relationship where you may be expecting mutual trust. Other relationships, such as work relationships, can also be impaired. Most people like to think of themselves as trustworthy, and/or trusted until proven different. But some uptight people just cannot get to that point. Others in their world have the impossible job of proving their trustworthiness, but can never fully achieve this, nor can the uptight person ever relax and trust first. No matter what you do to earn their trust, it is not sufficient.

Most difficult to cope with are your feelings when you continually encounter their mistrust exhibited by behaviors such as those listed above. You may adopt the attitude that you must try harder, or the attitude that your efforts to prove your trustworthiness are futile, and you no longer care or try to meet their demands. Neither attitude enriches or supports the relationship. If the relationship is an intimate one, tender and loving feelings can become eroded, leading to a much less satisfying relationship. You cannot change their deeply ingrained lack of trust, and this may be hard to accept.

## ENCOURAGEMENT AND SUPPORT

Needless to say, if the uptight person withholds approval and appreciation, he/she are also most likely to withhold encouragement and support. Indeed, some may even be discouraging and non-supportive, which are very detrimental to relationships whether intimate or other. The uptight person, of course, doesn't see it as withholding or as being discouraging and non-supportive. If you were to charge them as such, they would likely respond that they are trying to be realistic and to prevent your disappointment if things don't work out to your benefit. While some or all of what they present may be true, and it can be better to be aware of this, they do not also include some measure of encouragement and support along with the negative possibilities.

What is the value of encouragement and support? Encouragement conveys the following:

- Faith in your abilities and competency
- A desire to see you expand and develop
- Belief in your self-efficacy
- Reinforcement for your commitment to the endeavor

Support conveys the following:

- A willingness to assist you to accomplish your goals
- Belief in the worth of your endeavor
- That you are valued and appreciated
- A foundation of approval and acceptance for you as a separate person

Encouragement and support provide many positive things, so that when these are withheld, a valuable contribution to the relationship is compromised.

Notice that encouragement and support are more about you as a person than they are about what you are doing or the goal. This is because it is possible to be encouraging and supportive even when you disagree with what the person is doing or what he/she proposes to do. You do not have to agree to convey your commitment to the relationship, and/or to him/her as a valued and worthwhile person. Of course, this is not intended to suggest that you be encouraging and supportive of self-destructive, illegal acts, or destructive acts toward others. These should be discouraged. What is meant here is to encourage and support expansion, enrichment, growth, and development of and for the person.

*Coping Strategies.* When you are in a relationship with the Austere Withholding type, and find that relationship-enhancing factors are being withheld, you may want to examine what you want and need in a relationship, and what personal needs you have that may be contributing to your distress. The first step would be to reflect on your need for approval, appreciation, tolerance, respect for differences, trust, and encouragement and support. It could be that you have an intense need for one or more of these that is related to your unresolved issues, unfinished business, and/or self-development, and that no one would be able to adequately fulfill these for you. If this is not the case, and you have modest and reasonable needs and expectations, then you have few options. Three are listed below:

- Stop expecting the uptight person to provide the withheld relationship enhancers
- Find other sources to provide you with external approval and so on
- Become more self-sufficient and provide these for yourself, thus relying more on your internal resources

## INDICES OF SELF-ABSORPTION

Self-absorbed people can have and exhibit several of the following behaviors and attitudes, and when the intensity and anxiety of the uptight person is added to these, they become even more emphasized and troubling to relationships. The Austere Withholding type can exhibit many of the following. Don't forget that the self-absorbed person is mainly unaware of having and/or exhibiting these.

- Expecting prompt obedience and compliance with their demands and wishes, even unspoken ones
- The strong desire and need for admiration, especially unconditional and continual admiration
- An entitlement attitude that expects others to always agree with them without dissent or any hint of disapproval
- The notion that others will perceive them as unique, special, and superior
- All others will meet their need and demand for perfection
- They are always entitled to receive preferential treatment
- Others will understand that they have the "right" answers, that their way is the only correct way, and so on
- Others are expected to respond empathically, but should not expect reciprocity
- They should never be criticized, blamed, or have their mistakes revealed

The expectation of *prompt obedience* in providing this type of uptight person with what he/she wants and needs is one of their least endearing traits, as others are expected to intuit these, or to read their minds and provide what is wanted or needed without the person having to verbalize these. Others in their world can hear things like, "You should have known that I wanted this (whatever it was)," or "You should have been able to guess what was needed," or "If you really cared you would have known to do (provide, etc.) what I needed."

This expectation that others will comply or be obedient can be seen in their actions such as snide negative comments, sulking, nonverbal displays of anger, and open challenges about others' competence and commitment.

Having to cope with such an expectation can be very challenging, since it is unlikely that anyone will be able to intuit what is wanted or needed much of the time, no matter how close and intimate the relationship may be. Even the most loving and caring mother cannot do this all of the time for her beloved infant, and this is usually the closest relationship or best opportunity anyone has for this to happen.

It is futile to try to meet this expectation as it cannot be met, and you will continue to frustrate yourself and/or to feel inadequate.

The Austere Withholding type can have some traits and accomplishments that are admirable, but he/she can also expect *admiration* for everything about him/her all of the time. While everyone would appreciate some admiration some of the time, most people can be content with that and not expect it continually from everyone, or become upset when it is not forthcoming. The uptight person can do the following in his/her quest for admiration:

- Frequent self-nominations for awards and other recognitions
- Fish for compliments
- Boast and brag so that others realize how wonderful they are, and can compliment them
- Emphasize a minor mistake or the like to a point where others feel compelled to balance it out with a compliment
- Faintly praise another person to have an opportunity to tell how he/she is superior to that person
- Continually point out how he/she is morally superior, upright, and so on

This need for constant reassurance of value, superiority, and worth can also be accompanied by some contempt for others who are then perceived as inferior for not being as admirable as is the uptight person in his/her view. Some uptight people are able to disguise it better than others are, but even when it is disguised the attitude can be revealed in their subtle put-downs of others, statements of moral superiority, and so on.

*Agreement without dissent* means that others are expected to be in sync with whatever this person says or proposes, and to not openly disagree with his/her opinions, values, perspectives, demands, and so on. When there is considerable undeveloped narcissism, others are not clearly perceived as being separate and distinct from him/her, and thus are under his/her control. This means that if the uptight person has a perspective, opinion, and so on, then it must be so, and others cannot have an independent view. Their psychological boundaries have no ending, and others' boundaries have no beginning. Further, the very notion that someone disagrees is very threatening as that suggests to them that they are not fully in control, that they may be wrong, and/or that they are shameful in some way. It is these feelings and thoughts that can fuel the aggressive and/or negative reactions and responses when others disagree. The expectation may be unconscious, but still affects their thoughts and feelings about their self, and the role that others are to play in their lives.

*Unique, special, and superior* are how others are expected to view the self-absorbed person. Do not be fooled if they present more from the impoverished self perspective than from the grandiose self perspective, which generally happens with the Austere Withholding type. Both the impoverished and the grandiose perspectives assume that the person is unique, special, and superior, and that this is so evident that others should not fail to recognize and salute this in them. While everyone can appreciate being thought of this way at times and for specific accomplishments and characteristics, they are not expecting this at all times and for everything about them, as can some self-absorbed people.

When you are in a relationship with such a person, you are not expected to ever falter in viewing him/her as unique, special, and superior. In addition, you are expected to communicate this perspective both verbally and nonverbally through actions such as the following:

- Adoring looks at him/her
- Hanging on to his/her every word
- Comments about his/her uniqueness, specialness, and superiority
- To even make negative comments and/or put-downs about others as being inferior to him/her
- Convey that you have an unquestioned assumption that he/she is correct about everything
- Be prepared to express unwavering support and admiration

The self-absorbed person's *expecting and demanding perfection from others* can be very exhausting and frustrating for those in any kind of relationship with him/her. Such expectations and demands are unrealistic, unreasonable, and illogical as perfection is a goal to be worked for with the understanding that it can seldom be achieved, and that striving for attainment is the best that one can do. The Austere Withholding type of person can be diligent about pointing out imperfections and mistakes; commenting about lack of effort or commitment that produces less than perfection; and in communicating disappointment when his/her standards and criteria for perfection are not met. It appears that nothing you do is ever quite good enough no matter how hard you try, and knowing this can erode your self-confidence, self-esteem, and the quality of the relationship. While you also want perfection, you are more realistic and accepting of less than perfection and do not blame others for not always being able to attain it.

*Entitlement to preferential treatment* is an unconscious attitude for some self-absorbed people. Since attitudes are indirectly visible through words and actions, it can take time to become aware that this is an expectation as it is not directly expressed. These people expect or do things like the following that indicates the entitlement attitude:

- Refuse to wait in line
- Are impatient with taking turns
- Look for recognition and praise for practically everything they do
- Insist that their needs, wishes, and desires receive priority
- Push to get "their way" when choosing or deciding
- Think that they should receive more than others as they deserve more
- Feel that they should not have to meet the same criteria, standards, and the like as do others

Openly challenging any of these attitudes will not have positive outcomes, as the challenged person is unaware of his/her preferential need expectation, and is likely to feel attacked. Challenging them will only make a bad situation worse.

Uptight people can have a deeply held conviction that they have the "right answers" for just about everything. Don't be fooled by their declarations about not having all the answers or the right answers, as these declarations are only on the surface. They may really consciously believe what they say, but unconsciously know that they are right and that they do have the answers. They may have learned from past experiences that others do not appreciate their "right answers," and so they preface their remarks with the disclaimer. Not only are they unconsciously or consciously convinced that they have the right answers, they also expect others to recognize the "rightness," and also adopt and act on these. These are the people who will openly say, "I told you so," when others do not adopt and act on their answers, or they will indirectly convey the same message, and both can be accompanied with an air of smugness. Their smugness can be irritating, but just as they are unaware of the impact of their attitudes and behaviors on others, they do not notice the irritation, and/or dismiss it as envy of them.

Uptight people, especially those that fall into the Austere Withholding type, *will seldom or never respond empathically* to others. If they should appear to be empathic sometimes, it is because either they know the appropriate words, or they have involuntarily "caught" the emotion. They are usually better at sending emotions than they are at catching these, but it cannot be ruled out.

If they should "catch" someone's emotion, the responses they provide do capture the other person's feelings but these are experienced as their personal feelings, not the other person's feelings, keeping the focus on the self of the uptight person. What could have been an understanding of the other person is now a focus and emphasis on him/herself.

An important expectation of uptight people is that they should *never be criticized, blamed, or the like,* and this type may be especially sensitive to this. It doesn't just apply to having other people around to hear the criticism, it also applies when there are only the two of you. Any hint that they are less than perfect cannot be tolerated, no matter how mild or trivial it may be. Not only does this interfere with their grandiose perceptions of their self, it also allows the impoverished ego to surface with all of those negative self-perceptions and fears of inadequacy, and of being fatally flawed. It's no wonder that they do not want to experience these feelings, and will take immediate steps to prevent or to counteract them.

What you can experience in these situations is an attack on you, about your real or imaginary flaws, motives, inadequacies, and the like. All of a sudden you are put in a position where you feel you must answer their charges, explain, defend yourself, or apologize to him/her for something, the nature of which you are not clear about. You are caught off-guard, floundering, having confusing and frustrating feelings, and not understanding what could have precipitated this. The original subject of the conversation is now lost, blurred, and/or confounded. You did not understand that the uptight person would have such a violent reaction to something you thought was trivial, inconsequential, or mild.

## GENERAL TENDENCIES

The Austere Withholding type can exhibit the following tendencies:

- A very narrow range of interests and feeling expression
- Lack of empathy

- Grandiosity coupled with the impoverished ego, and entitlement attitudes and behaviors
- Arrogance, contempt, and other strong feelings about others and their worth
- Demonstrate negative and unwavering evaluations about others and what they should or ought to be

The constriction of the Austere Withholding type can be seen in their very narrow range of interests and feeling expression. Since these are very different, they will be discussed separately.

A narrow range of interests can be limiting to cognitive, social, and other kinds of development. Learning new things, meeting and getting to know people and sharing their interests, and having healthy and constructive new experiences can be enriching. However, when these are voluntarily or involuntarily restricted, growth and development can become stunted. This is not to say that someone should be interested in everything and everyone, but the idea is that having too limited interests is restrictive to other parts of one's life and enjoyment. The Austere Withholding type tends to have very limited interests, doesn't want to extend him/herself to learn new and different things, can only be interested in others who share his/her interests and thereby limits the extent of social contact and interactions, and is very resistant to trying new, healthy, and constructive experiences.

A narrow range of emotional expression is one of the characteristics that can be found in self-absorbed people. They generally express only some variations of anger and fear, the two primitive emotions that everyone seems to possess at birth. Some can use words for other emotions, but do not have the feelings that accompany the words. In one way, the Austere Withholding type does not withhold emotions. They have such a narrow range and depth of emotions that they really cannot access and express many of these. It could be helpful for the relationship to not expect or push for a range and depth of emotional expression from a person of this type. They do not have them, and cannot express them.

Lack of empathy is also a characteristic found in self-absorbed people, and can be a tendency of the Austere Withholding type. They want and can even demand that others be empathic with them, but there is no reciprocity. This tendency can be very troubling in any kind of relationship, but is especially so in an intimate relationship where mutual empathy is enriching. To give empathy, but to not receive it in return, can lead to diminished feelings of self-worth, increased feelings of inadequacy and of not being good enough, and finally to feelings of frustration and futility.

Adults can have expectations that other adults can be empathic, and when that does not occur, can then think that this absence is deliberate and voluntary on the part of the other person. If you are dealing with a self-absorbed person, especially one who has a Destructive Narcissistic Pattern (Brown, 1998), that person did not develop to the point where he/she can be emphatic, as this is a characteristic of healthy adult narcissism and that person is at an earlier stage in his/her narcissistic development. The Austere Withholding type of uptight people can fit this description for lack of empathy. They probably do not deliberately withhold empathy, they simply cannot be empathic and can become very angry if you were to challenge them or insist on receiving empathy from them. They cannot give you what they do not have.

Grandiosity coupled with the impoverished ego and entitlement attitudes are seen in this type by their deeply held convictions about what is right, wrong, good, and bad, and in their willingness to impose these perceptions on others by frequently telling them what they should or ought to do. They withhold emotional expression and lack empathy, but they also strongly contribute their moral convictions and assumptions that others should be more like them. They push to have their convictions accepted, for others to comply and act in accord with what they deem to be right and good, and to agree with what they consider as wrong and bad.

While their grandiosity can be easier to discern, do not forget that the impoverished ego is also present and may surface at any nanosecond. You may find it appearing at any hint of disagreement about the validity of their deeply held convictions, such as when you present a different perspective. You may think that you are just presenting alternatives and possibilities, but what they perceive is that you are telling them that they are wrong, flawed, and shameful. In order to maintain their grandiose self, they suppress the impoverished ego with anger at you for even suggesting that they are not absolutely correct, and can go on the offensive, or become even more withdrawn and sulk. You weren't getting much or anything in the way of empathy and emotional expression, but now you also have to cope with their anger and further withdrawal from the relationship.

The Austere Withholding type, in accord with their moral certainty of having the "correct" way and answers, can exhibit arrogance, contempt, and other strong feelings about others and their worth. Examples for behaviors that illustrate this tendency include the following:

- Saying, "I would (could) never do anything like what __ did, as that is just plain wrong," when someone makes a mistake, erroneous decision, or the like. It was not said in response to a legal matter or societal moral violation
- Making derogatory comments about people who differ from them in socioeconomic status, religion, race or ethnicity, disability, gender, or sexual orientation, and/or place of national origin
- Telling others that they would be better off if they did whatever he/she decreed that they should or ought to do
- Refusing to acknowledge the accomplishments and achievements of others, and pointing out how these were probably not earned or deserved
- Commenting about others' lack of worth, including put-downs, and other negative remarks about a person's moral and ethical principles, their native abilities and competencies, and/or their genetic personality traits

Coupled with the above behaviors and attitudes can also be evaluations of others that are generally and mostly negative about how these others are failing to be and do what they should or ought to be and do. They seldom have any approval for others that does not also include some reference to their perceived deficiencies. For example, let's suppose that someone graduated from college. The Austere Withholding type of uptight person would tend to make comments such as, "It's about time he graduated," or "It's a wonder that he managed to graduate, or "I wonder who he bribed to get the grades to graduate." They can be very judgmental and evaluative of others.

# 6

# Wallowing in Greed and Excess: The Indulgent and Entitled Type

At the other end of the spectrum from the Austere Withholding type is the Indulgent and Entitled type. The first one is sparse, miserly, and fears losing everything to the point where nothing is relinquished except only under extreme circumstances and grudgingly so, while the second is expansive, overly indulgent of personal wishes and desires, and feels entitled to get and take whatever he/she wants. However, they do have some attributes in common, such as the following:

- Withholding of affection, information, approval, acceptance, respect, and so on
- Expecting compliance and agreement from others
- Admiration seeking
- Controlling and micromanaging
- Contemptuous and superior attitude

But, there are also major differences. The Indulgent and Entitled type can display many of the following behaviors and attitudes:

- Attention seeking behavior, such as grand entrances and exits, loud voices, interrupting others as they speak
- Expansive and/or flamboyant gestures, speech, clothing, and other material possessions
- Boasting and bragging under the guise of social talk, or providing information
- Seeks flattery, compliments, and so on

- Bullies others to get his/her way, or whatever is desired
- Does not see any reason to deny him/herself what is wanted
- Can never admit mistakes or errors, rationalizes that others caused these
- Easily frustrated and annoyed when others fail to comply with demands, wishes, and so on
- Quick to attack as a defense; can be aggressive and overwhelming
- Most likely over indulges—such as food, alcohol, shopping, and/ or gambling
- Could be described as a workaholic

These are some of the behaviors and attitudes that can be troubling to others in relationships, especially when these are accompanied with intensity and anxiety. These behaviors and attitudes reflect considerable self-absorption, an inability to perceive others as separate from him/her as worthwhile individuals, and suggest a childish and more primitive level of inner emotional development. All of this can make interactions and relationships difficult. You are expecting someone with adult development, and are constantly confronted with someone who has the behaviors, attitudes, responses, and emotional expressions of a frustrated, angry child. Trying to understand and empathize with someone of this type only leaves you feeling bewildered and upset, and can even lead to self-doubt. Let's explore the behaviors and attitudes in the list.

**ATTENTION-SEEKING BEHAVIOR**

Without attention, this type can experience extreme anxiety, and because of this feeling can go to extensive measures to make sure that attention to him/her never flags or ceases. They want to stand out, and most often, they do. There are numerous ways to bring and keep attention on oneself. Complete the following exercise to see if you use any of these, and if the uptight person in your world uses them. Rate both yourself and the other person using the designated scale.

**Exercise 6.1**
**Attention-seeking Behaviors**

   5–Always or almost always
   4–Very often

3–Frequently
2–Seldom
1–Never or almost never

1. Wait to be asked to participate or for input      5 4 3 2 1

2. Say challenging, provocative things, and then back off 5 4 3 2 1

3. Interrupt others and/or finish their sentences      5 4 3 2 1

4. Dress in ways that bring attention to oneself      5 4 3 2 1

5. Talk loudly      5 4 3 2 1

6. Forcibly express your opinions and/or
   disagreements      5 4 3 2 1

7. Become wounded, insulted, or offended and sulk      5 4 3 2 1

8. Make grand and sweeping gestures      5 4 3 2 1

9. Enter and/or exit in a noisy way      5 4 3 2 1

10. Procure and use showy material possessions
   (jewelry, cars, houses, antiques, and the like)      5 4 3 2 1

Scoring and interpretation: Add to ratings to obtain a total score for each of you.

| 43–50 | Exhibits considerable attention seeking behaviors always or almost always |
| 35–42 | Exhibits lots of attention seeking behaviors frequently |
| 27–34 | Exhibits some attention seeking behaviors often |
| 19–26 | Exhibits attention-seeking behaviors on occasion |
| 10–18 | Exhibits few if any attention seeking behavior |

If the rating of yourself totaled 30 or above, you may want to think about moderating many of the listed or similar attention seeking behaviors and try to reduce their frequency. If the total rating for the uptight person in your life is 30 or above, you can only try to understand the goal for their behavior, that of ensuring that they continue to exist. It is that validation that they seek from others, and they do not have sufficient inner resources to provide that validation.

## EXPANSIVE GESTURES

Performers learn how to move, stand, and gesture so as to capture the audience's attention. Even when standing still, they can still "upstage" others and lessen any attention to them. Many Indulgent and Entitled types are able to do this without specific lessons, and one way is through the use of expansive gestures.

Expansive gestures are those that take up more space and time than is usual. These gestures can impinge on others' personal space, are calculated to keep the attention, and can convey a sense of the person's importance. For example, these are the people who spread their possessions over a wide area of a table at a meeting, not just in front of the chair where they will sit. When talking, they swing their arms and move their hands to emphasize points, but these also can have the effect of moving into other's personal space. Other examples of expansive gestures include the following:

- Walking down a sidewalk or corridor in the middle, and not moving aside for on-coming traffic
- Hugging and pulling others close to them in greeting when they don't know the other person well or at all, or having any sense of how they feel about hugs
- Doing something to draw attention to themselves when others are talking
- Exaggerating nonverbal signals of emotions, such as sadness or excitement
- Sending unmistakable signs of boredom or disinterest when others are talking; moving and shifting impatiently
- Exaggerated swing of the hips when walking, or stomping loudly
- Entering or exiting a room noisily, rapidly, and with emphasis
- Using voice tones that are loud, even in close quarters, or when with a few people
- Dressing in clothing that is revealing, or inappropriate for the circumstances; or clothing that is excessively tight, or cut to emphasize erotic body parts or zones

Expansive gestures are a subset of attention seeking behavior, but some also have the additional goals of securing admiration and/or of being considered as unique and special. The person is seeking external validation of existence and worth, and can never be reasonably assured or convinced of these. Most of these people are probably not aware of these needs, or what they are doing to meet them. Trying to make them aware or providing reassurance will not work and are not sufficient. You can never fill the void, as they can never get enough of these from others.

## BOASTING AND BRAGGING

The real messages for boasting and bragging are to reinforce the person's superiority and others' inferiority. These people are saying, "Look and marvel at how wonderful I am, but you are not." While it can be encouraging to be proud of one's achievements and accomplishments, when this is taken to extremes, it becomes more arrogance and contempt than realistic pride. Boasting and bragging are other ways uptight people seek reassurance, and these acts also reduce their anxiety.

These people are drawn to others who can continually provide them with opportunities to showcase their superiority while, also directly or indirectly, showing that others are inferior. Conversely, they avoid and reject anyone who doesn't provide these opportunities or show signs of lagging in admiration for them, and maybe even denigrate anyone who doesn't appear to think they are as wonderful as they think they are.

A major consideration to keep in mind is that their boasting and bragging are almost continual, with few conversations with them that don't produce some of these. It's not an infrequent occurrence as can happen with anyone who is pleased with a personal accomplishment or achievement, or with that of someone close to them, such as a child or spouse. The frequency and the attitude are clues to excessive needs for attention and admiration.

If you want to continue a cordial relationship with this person, you will find it helpful to try not to exhibit disinterest, a more realistic and balanced perspective, or do anything that would indicate that you find the boasting and/or bragging tiresome or tacky. The uptight person is desperately seeking validation through these means, even though he/she may be doing so on an unconscious level. Any hint of disagreement or disinterest will be perceived as an attempt to destroy the person, will be vigorously fought off, and you will be rejected. Refrain from acts such as:

- Pointing out where he/she did not do this alone, others were helpful
- Suggesting that circumstances favored him/her
- Changing the topic
- Trying to interject another story
- Downplaying what was achieved or done

- Saying you admire someone who did something similar to what the uptight person did
- Identifying where he/she has an advantage over others
- Telling them that they are boasting or bragging
- Saying nothing

If you want to keep them cordial and approving of you, do one or more of the following:

- Be enthusiastic about whatever it is they are boasting or bragging about
- Act as a cheerleader, boosting your team
- Ask them to tell you more about it, and listen intently
- Bring it up again later in the interaction
- Call other people to join you to hear about it
- Remark on it at a later date and say how outstanding he/she is

## SEEKS FLATTERY AND COMPLIMENTS

While boasting and bragging are ways to seek flattery and compliments, there are other ways this type can use, such as having an expectation that others will provide these spontaneously, not just in response to being told of an achievement or accomplishment. Uptight people of this type can expect to be flattered and complimented on a variety of things, and each can have different expectations. For example, some may like to have their appearance noted and be complimented, others may want their ordinary activities flattered, while some others may preen when flattered on just existing.

What can be worth noting in your relationship with this type is how interactions proceed when you don't provide compliments and/or flattery every time. Reflect on a recent interaction where you did not flatter or compliment this person, or did not do so in a pleasing way. He/she could have been abrupt, withdrew from the interaction either physically or emotionally, challenged or attacked you about something, made a disparaging remark about you or someone else, and/or turned to talk with someone else. Now, reflect on an interaction when you did present an acceptable compliment or flattery. Most likely, you received his/her attention, he/she acted pleased, the conversation continued and was pleasant or even jovial, you may have received a compliment in return, and you both left feeling pleased. What a contrast! If you want to maintain the second scenario, be sure to constantly and continually compliment and flatter this type.

Preserving your integrity can get to be a challenge when you try to provide the desired compliments and flattery. You don't want to be insincere or lie, but you don't always see something that you feel needs complimenting. Try the following to generate ideas for what to say when you face this dilemma so as not to lead to negative consequences:

1. Begin with generating a mental list of the person's most positive attributes, such as the following examples; unique, hard worker, confident, have a different way of looking at things, have a warm smile, are reliable, and the like.
2. Next, mentally form a sentence that uses the complimentary phrase, and adds an explanation to it. For example, "You have a warm smile that makes me feel welcome (brightens up the day)."

Let's suppose that they are fishing for a compliment about what they are wearing, but you don't like it. You could compliment the color or fit without giving away your dislike. The strategy is to find a way to phrase your comments so that you both compliment the person, and preserve your integrity.

## BULLIES OTHERS

Some Indulgent and Entitled types can also be bullies, and other types can also exhibit bullying behavior, but this type can be worse. Their self-absorption permits them to assume that they are superior and others are inferior; they are entitled to get what they want and when they want it; others exist only to serve them and gratify their needs; and that others are extensions of them and under their control. These behaviors and attitudes can be very frustrating and infuriating. Let's take a look at some behaviors and attitudes that can signal you are being bullied:

- They coerce you to do things you do not want to do, or which are not in your best interest.
- They are quick to point out any perceived weaknesses or inadequacies they feel you have.

- Not only do they lie and speculate about others, they also encourage you to do the same.
- Whatever happens is not their fault, and you and others seem to get some or all of the blame.
- They work to exclude and/or isolate you, such as not notifying you when others are notified, not giving you information, and the like.
- They snoop and spy on you and others.
- Some can be loudly critical of anything about you in an attempt to embarrass you in front of others.
- They spread lies and distortions about you behind your back, and then term you overly sensitive or misinformed if you challenge them.
- You experience constant and continual criticism, fault finding, nitpicking, and the like.
- You are undermined, especially when there is an audience.
- You are subjected to belittling, denigrating, disparaging remarks about yourself.
- He/she encourages you to feel guilty and at fault.

If you experience some or most of these, you may want to take steps to protect yourself. The best strategy is to get away from a bully, but that is not always feasible or possible. The next best strategy is to improve your psychological boundary strength so that you resist the assaults, do not incorporate them into your self and trigger feelings of guilt or shame, and are able to be strong and resilient. However, building your psychological boundaries takes time and effort. Some suggestions are provided in later chapters, and working with a competent therapist can expedite this growth. Some short term coping strategies include the following:

- Limit the amount of personal information you disclose to this type. Don't give them material they can use to your disadvantage.
- Don't confide your problems, concerns, hunches, etc., to them or to others who are close to them.
- Don't laugh or even seem to agree with their disparaging remarks or other put-downs about you.
- Maintain your emotional balance and equanimity.
- Do not challenge or confront them as that will only intensify the bullying behavior.

- Correct lies and other misinformation as soon as possible, but not with this person. Do so with others who are bringing this to your attention, or who are repeating what they heard.
- Ignore the behavior as much as possible.

## INDULGENT

Excessive indulgences, especially those that are destructive to the person and to their relationships, and/or are financially irresponsible characterize this type. Worse is that they also feel entitled to do and/or to attain these, that others should assist or comply with their efforts, and that they should suffer no negative consequences. Efforts to make them aware of what they are doing that is counterproductive do not work as they may be cognitively aware of the negative acts and consequences, but they do not accept these on an emotional or psychological level. Their self-absorbed behaviors and attitudes of grandiosity, arrogance, contempt, having to be considered as unique and special, and other such behaviors and attitudes will not permit them to be aware of the negative effects of their indulgence(s) and entitlement attitude. Central and essential for your understanding of the excessive indulgences is the deep needs these fulfill to keep them from experiencing the internal emptiness at the core of their self, and the constant and continual anxiety waiting to overwhelm and consume them the instant they let their guard down.

The self-destructive aspects of their indulgences can be severe. For example, indulging in the desire to acquire material goods, such as pricy antiques, can lead to their spending funds excessively, and even using funds that are needed for necessities. The self-destructive aspects for substance use or abuse, such as alcohol abuse, can carry medical, relational, and financial consequences that are debilitating to the person. The uptight person can have a cognitive or intellectual understanding of the self-destructiveness of his/her indulgences, but does not appear to be able to use that knowledge in constructive ways that are helpful for him/her. The deep affective understanding seems to be lacking, as is the empathy for others affected by his/her destructive behavior.

And so, this type continues to indulge with an internal conviction that there is nothing really wrong with what they are doing, it's under control and can be stopped at any time, but that it is really a necessity. There is no reason in their minds, for denial of their indulgences. Nothing you do or say will get through this denial, and your efforts to take care of them are futile.

## NO REASON FOR PERSONAL DENIAL

Overly indulgent is one defining characteristic for this type, and their indulgences are sought and carried out with just as much fervor and intent as is the miserliness of the Austere and Withholding type, just in the opposite direction. Self-sacrifice for any reason is not an option and the conviction that they are entitled, more worthy and deserving, and that their wishes and needs should receive priority do not allow for the possibility of denying oneself indulgences for the benefit of others. Further, engaging in attaining and having the indulgences keeps their anxiety under control and fears at bay, especially for anxieties and fears around personal inadequacies. Since anxiety and fear are constant companions for them, the need to be indulgent can be taken to extremes, and may be self-destructive.

However dire the consequences, this type will continue to overindulge. No amount of telling, selling, begging, or threatening will get through the defense of denial. Logic and reason do not work either. They have the deep conviction that what they are doing is worthwhile, is necessary for their comfort and pleasure, is not hurtful to others, and is not destructive. They want it, they enjoy it, and see no reason why they cannot have it. They can even go to extremes to get whatever it is, no matter the monetary or personal cost to themselves or to others.

## NEVER ADMITS MISTAKES

Making mistakes is so very painful and shaming that uptight people, especially this type, cannot bring themselves to admit making any. Listen very carefully when someone you think fits the uptight description seems to admit making a mistake. Usually they will either continue to talk and rationalize that no one could have avoided the mistake because of circumstances not under their control, or they will find a reason to blame someone else for the mistake, or will declare that there was no mistake. They never accept responsibility for their mistakes.

Worse is when they blame you or someone else for even surfacing the mistake, and/or berate you for not preventing it, or they fantasize that you have a malicious intent to shame and hurt him/her. It becomes your fault that he/she is even associated with the mistake, and that is intolerable for the person. The Indulgent and Entitled type can then become aggressive and attacking, and/or vengeful, where the focus is shifted from the original mistake to how inadequate and shameful anyone else is for even suggesting that he/she could make a mistake. Others, including you, can then be put on the defensive, and even begin to feel guilty.

If, or when, you find yourself in similar circumstances with someone who does not or cannot admit making mistakes, and who is offloading any blame or responsibility, you may find it helpful to do the following:

- Don't try to get them to admit making a mistake. Such admissions may not seem to be a big deal for you, and the mistake may be minor or of little consequence, but this is a really big deal for that person.
- Try to manage and contain your anger and hurt if you are blamed. Don't accept the blame or apologize, just make a neutral or noncommittal response to try and defuse the situation.
- Give soothing responses such as no one has ever found a way to prevent all mistakes, or it's not important.
- Ignore it.

## EASILY FRUSTRATED

Intense and anxious people can often be easily frustrated, and if they have considerable self-absorption also, then they can stay frustrated almost all of the time. This happens because they can perceive others as extensions of their self, and therefore, under their control. It's as if you can't control what a part of you is doing, and this is very frustrating. Since other people are separate and are individuals, they most often do what they want to do, but not necessarily what the uptight person wants or expect them to do. Some can even be frustrated by objects, by their inability to be perfect in all things and at all times, when events and situations don't go as planned, and at anything that doesn't meet their expectations or needs.

Frustration is a common emotion, and almost everyone has experienced some frustration. However, many people have learned to handle their frustration so that it doesn't overwhelm them, or negatively affect every aspect of their lives, and they become realistic about their personal limitations so that they don't expect perfection all of the time.

They are more accepting of their inadequacies, flaws, and personal limitations. On the other hand, the self-absorption of uptight people does not permit them to develop these kinds of coping mechanisms.

You cannot prevent frustrations for someone else, especially for this type. Yes, you can do everything in your power to ensure that things run smoothly, there are no glitches or unexpected surprises, or that you anticipate possible frustrating events so as to keep him/her from becoming frustrated. This work involves a lot of your time and effort, and still there is a high probability of failure where something else frustrates the person. Your challenge is to recognize your personal limitations and responsibilities, as the person is an adult and responsible for him/herself, to accept that he/she is in charge of his/her emotions and not you, and to accept the person as is, recognizing that the ease of frustration he/she experiences is a part of his/her self. Further, you don't have to accept the blame and criticism for someone else's frustration. When you feel guilty or embarrassed, this signals that you are accepting some or all of the blame and criticism, that you don't recognize the limits of your personal responsibility for another person's emotions, and that you are buying into his/her perceptions of your personal inadequacy. Building your psychological boundary strength and self-confidence can help you recognize and accept the difference between what is yours and what is the other person's.

## QUICK TO ATTACK

The same characteristics that lead to this type's bullying behavior play major roles in the tendencies to be quick to attack as a defense. Attacks can assume many forms, such as the following:

- Unwarranted or invalid blame or criticism
- Shouting at you
- Saying things to humiliate you
- Nit-picking and fault finding
- Offensive language directed at you
- Taunting and/or teasing you as a means to embarrass you
- Using sarcasm
- Trying to trigger your fear, anger, guilt, and/or shame
- Unpleasant, threatening, or harassing calls, e-mails, texts, and the like
- Fomenting rumors and lies about you

These attacks can have one or more goals: power, control, manipulation, to shore up their impoverished self, to prevent awareness of an inadequate self, to prevent others from seeing the flawed and shameful self, and/or revenge. The specific goal(s) for a specific person may be difficult to discern as many are primarily unconscious where the uptight person is not aware of his/her motives or goals. Regardless of the goal, the usual responses of the person being attacked are to be on the defensive, hurt, and experiencing many uncomfortable feelings. The responses permit the uptight person to accomplish his/her goal, which, in turn, reinforces the attacking behavior. The attacked person is left with many residual feelings, and can become wary and cautious of the uptight person. Some may try harder to please him/her only to experience more attacks because they work, and the uptight person's goal is accomplished. Trying to prevent or handle these attacks seems futile because whatever the attacked person tries does not work, and they continue to suffer the negative responses from the attacking behavior.

Since the self-absorption of this type has the firm conviction that he/she is entitled to go on the offensive, to control and/or manipulate others, to point out just how inadequate and flawed others are, and to increase personal feelings of superiority, any appeals to this person to cease, to modify their attacking behavior, or to be aware and sensitive of the impact of their attacks on others will fail. Confrontation is not advised as what is likely to happen is that an even more intense attack will be mounted in retaliation, making bad matters worse.

What are some strategies that have a possibility of success? First off, you need to define success as something other than getting the uptight person to change and stop attacking. Nothing you do or say will cause this to happen, nor will it influence him/her to consider changing. He/she doesn't perceive the attacks as "wrong," and so is not open to altering the behavior. There is one exception, and that is in the workplace, where a more powerful boss or supervisor can demand and get some behavioral changes. But even that is limited as the uptight person can continue to use some of the more indirect ways to attack, such as spreading rumors and lies. Outside the workplace, there is no one who can demand or enforce behavior changes.

There are some strategies that can provide relief for you:

- Build your self and your psychological boundary strength so that your feelings of guilt or shame do not become triggered by his/

her accusations, criticisms, blame, and so on. Their goal will not then be met and their behavior is not reinforced.

- Refuse to engage either by standing your ground and responding calmly, or by just walking away. Take charge of your emotions. You can decide whether or not to feel humiliated. Just because that is their intent, doesn't mean you have to buy into it.
- Ignore acts like nit-picking, fault finding, taunting, and teasing. Change the subject to something more important.
- Walk away from offensive language. Do not use it in retaliation.
- Sarcasm is an indirect way to express feelings, and you can try to identify what feelings the other person has that are being expressed through sarcasm. You can decide if you want to respond to the indirectly expressed feelings, and ignoring is also an option.
- Determine what options you have, such as legal, policy, and the like, to address electronic harassment, and use these.
- You cannot prevent lies, rumors, and so on, so your best options are to not participate in these acts against others, and to correct any lies or misinformation about you when these are brought to your attention.

Try to refrain from mounting a direct attacking counteroffensive, or using the same tactics as does the uptight person. Doing these things will not present you in a positive way, and can backfire, as you are not as intense as the uptight person who must win at all costs. What is better to do in the long term is to become successful at what you do, have your meaningful and satisfying relationships, and to build your healthy adult self.

## WORKAHOLIC

Some indulgent and entitled people can also exhibit behavior associated with workaholics where their work assumes priority for their existence, and they go to extremes to fulfill their need to work. This is not just dedication to their work, and an understandable desire to succeed and be productive as that can be praiseworthy. With the workaholic, the task is never successful enough or completed to their satisfaction. These people can spend much or most of their time on work-related activities. Use the following scale to determine the extent to which you or the designated uptight person may exhibit workaholic behaviors.

**Exercise 6.2**

**Workaholic Scale**

*Directions*: Rate the degree to which the behavior is exhibited.

5–Always or almost always
4–Frequently
3–Sometimes
2–Seldom
1–Never or almost never

1. Spends more than the usual expected number of
   hour at work daily or weekly over one or more years  5  4  3  2  1

2. Sleeps very little with no underlying physical condition or medication to cause insomnia  5  4  3  2  1

3. Spends hours refining completed work  5  4  3  2  1

4. Cannot relax or enjoy hobbies or recreational
   activities  5  4  3  2  1

5. Leisure activities are work related, e.g., playing
   golf with prospective customers  5  4  3  2  1

6. Constantly seeks or develops work tasks to stay
   engaged in work  5  4  3  2  1

7. Uses work as an excuse to not participate or to limit
   participation in family or other relationship's activities  5  4  3  2  1

8. Sends numerous work related late night or early
   morning e-mail or text messages on a regular basis  5  4  3  2  1

9. Resists taking vacations from work  5  4  3  2  1

10. Frets about work when sick, on holidays, or
    when unable to get to work  5  4  3  2  1

Scoring: Add the rating to derive a total score. Use the following
descriptions to evaluate the rating.

| | |
|---|---|
| 43–50 | Exhibits most of the behaviors associated with workaholics |
| 35–42 | Exhibits many such characteristics frequently |
| 27–34 | May have some characteristics associated with worka-holics, but exhibits these infrequently |
| 19–26 | Has very few such characteristics and/or infrequently engages in them |
| 10–18 | Has none or only one such characteristic and/or never or almost never engages in these |

Scores of 35 and above can indicate that work is the central and driving force for the person. He/she may also be perceived as being very successful by many people, and the hard work may have paid off in terms of monetary and material goods. However, the person's sense of his/her existence is one-dimensional and, without the work, he/she has little or nothing that is meaningful or satisfying. Indeed, without work, the person is apt to become despairing and severely depressed.

Work is an escape from anxiety about oneself for this type. There the person is engaged, and uncomfortable thoughts and emotions are warded off, denied, and/or repressed. Doubts about personal adequacy, worth, and competencies can be kept at bay, and there is little or no danger that others will see their flaws since the work success can blind them to other less successful aspects of their self.

You have few or no strategies for coping with a workaholic. If the person is a boss, you can never live up to him/her, except to become as he/she is. If you were to try and do so, you would then most likely to be perceived by him/her as competition and reacted to in negative, undercutting ways. If the person is a spouse or lover, you will not be able to change him/her, and your only recourses are to leave, or accept and adjust—a very bleak outlook.

There are some actions you may want to avoid, as these will not be effective for changing the workaholic behavior, nor will there be positive effects on the relationship. You will not feel better, nor will you accomplish your aim or goals.

- Don't confront with the motive of trying to get him/her to acknowledge that his/her actions are having a negative effect on you and on the relationship. Your feelings are not this person's priority and they are likely to be ignored or discounted.
- Don't attempt to arouse guilt or shame. It will not work and may be turned around on you.
- Don't push for promises to change. Doing so shows that you don't understand their need to keep from feeling anxious.
- Don't bring other people into the discussion in an effort to validate your perceptions, and to support your wish for changes. This is likely to be perceived as "ganging up."
- Don't whine, carp, complain, nag, or cry. He/she can ignore this, or can outdo you.

# 7

# "You Will Do What I Want": The Controlling and Manipulative Type

The envy experienced by the Controlling and Manipulative type is all consuming and overwhelming for them; it is the driving force underlying many of their behaviors and attitudes. No matter how successful they may be, or what they achieve, they are still angry about others who they perceive as having something they want and deserve because they are superior. This envy causes them to work hard, to seek revenge especially on the envied ones, to use any means possible to attain what is wanted or desired, but is also a major reason for their dissatisfaction and lack of enjoyment for what they have and for what they have accomplished. Let's examine some of their more troubling behaviors.

**Exercise 7.1**

**Controlling and Manipulative Behaviors**

*Materials:* One or two sheets of paper, and a pen or pencil

*Directions:* Find a place to work where you will not be disturbed, and follow the described procedure.

1. Write the numbers 1–14 down the left side of the paper in a column, or look at the following list of descriptors and write the descriptor, such as sly. At the top of the page, label three columns: Yes, No, Not observed.

2. Look at the following list of descriptors and their definitions, and either check yes, no, or not observed for each descriptor for the uptight person in your life. Don't worry about the context for the particular behavior; check yes if they do engage in it at all.

| Descriptor | Definition |
| --- | --- |
| 1. Sly | Secretively underhanded |
| 2. Deceitful | Inclined to cheat or deceive, deliberately misleading |
| 3. Conniver | Plots, conspires, feigns ignorance |
| 4. Cheats | Deceives by trickery; swindles; practices fraud |
| 5. Steals | Obtains by theft, secretly or artfully |
| 6. Lies | Untruthful |
| 7. Competitive | Rivalry, strive for dominance, superiority |
| 8. Vindictive | Spiteful, inclined to be vengeful |
| 9. Exploitive | Uses selfishly or unethically |
| 10. Contemptuous | An attitude of bitter disdain or scorn |
| 11. Ruthless | Has no compassion or mercy |
| 12. Envy | Desires and resents what others have |
| 13. Coercive | Uses threats, intimidation, and/or pressure to dominate |
| 14. Vengeful | Seeks revenge for real or imagined insults, offenses, and the like |

3. Now, make a list of the behaviors and attitudes that you checked yes, and put a check mark by the descriptions that arouse the most intense negative feelings for you. List the feelings you experience when you think about or observe the uptight person engaging in the behavior(s) beside each descriptor.
4. Next, write a short sentence or paragraph about each of the intense negative feelings you experience that describes the experiencing and the impact on you. For example, suppose you listed anger as a feeling. A paragraph might be something like this.

*I got angry when I realized that he, once again, undermined me, and I could not prevent it, nor could I correct what he did. I was helpless and impotent and that made me even angrier.*

5. Read your sentences and/or paragraphs, and then write how your body feels when you experience each feeling, and how your body is reacting as you think and write about your feelings. Rate the intensity of each feeling as you are experiencing it right now. Rate them from 0–no intensity, to 10–as intense as it was when the event happened.
6. Reflect on each feeling rated as 6 or higher, e.g., anger. These are the negative effects you continue to carry with you; they continue to negatively affect and impact you physically, psychologically, emotionally, and most likely, in your relationships.

The Controlling and Manipulative behaviors have numerous negative effects on you and others. What this chapter emphasizes is how you can work to reduce or eliminate some or all of these effects. Also presented are expanded descriptors for the behaviors.

## SLY

People who are secretively underhanded are trying to gain an advantage, but the only way they see to do so is by using underhanded tricks to put others in a poor light. They are trying to be superior by ensuring that others are perceived as inferior. They say and do things that, on the face of it, appear to be positive, but these carry an edge and lots of negativity. Some examples follow:

- Wondering out loud something negative about a person, but has deniability of negative connotations if they are challenged about what was said
- Going to a superior or to someone near to a person, and telling them something negative about the person, asking them to keep it confidential; however, they have an expectation that it will be passed on to the person
- Goading others to repeat negative comments, rumors, and the like
- Starting unfounded rumors and speculations
- Preying on a person's weakness and/or sensitivity

Underlying the slyness can be doubts about oneself: efficacy, competency, worth, and the like. The sly person can have considerable insecurity, anxiety, and fear that the self is inadequate and fatally flawed. To overcome these doubts, fears, and flaws, they use any means available to undercut others and then shore up their self.

Because of the secretive nature of the underhanded acts, there are few strategies available to you. You can be in the position of always trying to remediate what was done, and that is usually ineffective. Further, you may not receive much understanding or support from others as they may not even recognize the underhandedness. Some options are as follows:

- Expect the behavior since you probably have sufficient evidence that he/she does this to you and others.
- Don't be too trusting of the person, rationalizing that he/she meant no harm.
- Work to build your self so that these acts don't hurt or arouse negative thoughts and feelings about your self. (Building strategies are provided in a later chapter.)
- Build your relationships so as to have encouragement and support when you experience the negative effects of his/her slyness.

## DECEITFUL

Somehow it is difficult to believe that anyone is deliberate in their deceitfulness even in the face of evidence to the contrary. We would rather believe that the person made an honest mistake, was ill or misinformed, did not have sufficient or the right information, but most of all, cared enough about us to not intentionally mislead or cheat us. What we fail to recognize or accept is that the person can be so intent and focused on him/herself, to the extent that we, or anyone else, don't have value for them if they see how deceit will help them gain an advantage or exhibit their dominance. Their self-absorption permits them to be indifferent to us as worthwhile, separate from them, individuals, and so we should be willing to be deceived if that is what they want or feel they need to do.

Deception has severe negative consequences for relationships; trust is eroded, feelings of hurt and betrayal emerge, persons can feel devalued and minimized, and there can be a blow to one's self-esteem as not being good enough. Reflect on a time where you were deceived and recall your feelings then and now, and changes to the relationship because of the deceit.

Coping with the deceitful person takes thought, time, and energy on your part as you have to take action to prevent being misled, rooked, and the like. These strategies can be helpful:

- Verify, verify, verify, especially if the information could possibly affect you in some way. Be discrete in asking around, but check it out.
- Take nothing they say at face value. Don't openly challenge what they say unless you have facts to the contrary, and then do so civilly and politely. Just remain skeptical about whatever they say.
- Determine needed or desired information for yourself, don't ask or rely on them to provide you information.
- Know workplace policies and procedures so as to not be misled.
- Stay alert.

### CONNIVER

Some people seem to delight in plots and conspiracies, especially those that get them what they want, and put others at a disadvantage. They plan long term and are very focused on their goals; such as besting others to cause them to lose; circumventing laws, policies, procedures, and the like; and are constantly working to achieve whatever is desired. All of this thought, time, and effort would be admirable if it were directed toward something positive, but it is directed toward achieving negative and less admirable goals. They can also seek to prevent others from achieving or getting something, and/or seek revenge for real or imagined offenses, but also feel that they are justified in what they do.

Most of the time, they enlist others in the plot or conspiracy, either with their agreement and knowledge, or by keeping them in the dark about the true goal. These others can be genuine in their participation and cooperation, but are more likely to have been manipulated to join in. Connivers can prey on people's greed, fears, desire for revenge, and other such negative needs and desires. They seldom recognize that they are being used to achieve the conniver's aims, and may not know what pay-off the conniver is seeking.

Uptight people who are connivers can be working to prevent what they fear, for example: destruction, abandonment, awareness of personal inadequacies, shame, and so on. These fears are deep-seated and have been with them for some time. These people never feel secure enough to trust anyone, and are always on the alert for real or fantasized plots and conspiracies against them. Imagine their inner world of utmost insecurity where they fantasize that the outer world is constantly seeking to attack and destroy them, and they either have insufficient or no inner resources to prevent the imagined destruction. They can neither trust themselves, nor anyone else.

There are few coping strategies to employ with connivers, and the best that you may be able to do is to stay out of the way.

- Stay alert for possible plots and conspiracies directed against you.
- Don't join in those directed against others.
- Learn to identify when you are being manipulated for someone else's purpose.

## CHEATING

Cheating is akin to deception with the addition of the methods: trickery, swindling, and fraud. Examples for cheating include the following:

- Not playing fair—games, sports, etc.
- Taking unearned credit for other's work
- Deceiving a spouse or partner about finances and/or having other intimate relationships
- Using, demanding, or hoarding more than your fair share of resources
- Not following or violating rules, regulations, policies, and the like
- Gaining an advantage, such as secretly moving your golf ball to a more favorable spot
- Copying from someone's paper or exam
- Submitting work completed by someone else

These are all means to gain an unfair advantage and to not have to accept responsibility.

Some people are so competitive, and losing is so shameful and painful for them that they go to extraordinary measures to "win." The ways to cheat at almost anything are so numerous, and people are so inventive, that it becomes almost impossible to prevent cheating. Just think about the extent to which schools and universities have gone to prevent academic dishonesty without success, as every time they manage to prevent one form, cheaters find or develop several new forms. It is still of major concern for our educational institutions.

Like other behaviors described so far in this chapter, there is little you can do to prevent cheating, especially with uptight people who feel entitled to get what they want by any means possible. Furthermore, suspicion of a spouse or intimate partner works negatively against the relationship. Either you trust him/her, or you stay tied up in knots wondering if he/she is cheating. About the only situation where you can take steps to prevent some cheating is in the workplace.

- Document your work and your ideas.
- When working with a team or work group, provide frequent written summaries and progress updates on your contributions, tasks, assignments, and so on.
- Be honest and trustworthy yourself, but don't necessarily expect this from others.
- Keep a record of meetings, impromptu conversations, e-mails, and phone calls about work related matters, especially those with the uptight person.
- Make a practice of getting your task assignments in writing when possible, from the boss or supervisor. Verify any tasks given or conveyed to you by a co-worker.

## STEALING

Akin to cheating, stealing can also be a tactic of this type. They don't necessarily steal material things much of the time, although some who have a need to hoard can steal goods, and some do steal costly material goods or money. The ones that we are most likely to encounter are those that are inclined to steal things like ideas and other people's creations, and/or to borrow things without returning them. Stealing is another way they take advantages that help them gain superiority. Examples of stealing include the following:

- Plagiarism
- Corporate espionage
- Hoarding office supplies and/or using these for non-work related purposes

- Using work equipment and services for personal concerns, such as e-mail, shopping, or personal phone calls
- Presenting someone's ideas as theirs
- Diverting money needed for family maintenance, such as using the mortgage payments for something personal and unnecessary
- Downloading and/or sharing music without paying for it
- Buying and selling knockoff designer goods

Some of these acts are so serious as to carry legal penalties and consequences, and some can have significant negative effects on relationships. Still others, such as using work materials and services for personal needs, are so common as to not be worthy of pursuing unless it becomes excessive. For example, most workplaces would not prosecute or have other negative penalties for taking some small amounts of office supplies.

Nevertheless, the uptight person perceives whatever he/she steals as an entitlement, whether that something is material or abstract, such as an idea or creation. There are few things that are so disconcerting, infuriating, and produce more feelings of impotence than the realization that someone stole your idea. You usually cannot prove that you had the idea first, nor can you prove to someone else's satisfaction that the other person usurped it. If you were to try and protest that you had the idea first, it would probably appear that you were trying to take credit away from that person. You lose either way, and are left to try and cope with your residual feelings.

Working with or for the Controlling and Mmanipulative type who steals can keep you on edge, wondering how you can protect yourself. About all that you can do is to act in honest ways yourself, try and protect theft of your possessions, and/or your ideas. Reporting thefts (ideas, material goods, services) doesn't usually work in your favor unless there are legal consequences for what was stolen. There are laws and other consequences for plagiarism, copyright violations and theft, but these can be difficult to document and prosecute. It's sad to say, but your best strategy for protection of your ideas is to keep them to yourself until you have them in some form, such as written and disseminated, where you can document that you are the creator. Don't discuss them with anyone that you have not found to be trustworthy, and even then you may need to be circumspect.

## LYING

Lies are deliberate untruths that erode trust, confidence, and relationships. They are intended to deceive and mislead for one's personal gain, for revenge or other intentions to hurt someone, and to protect the self from shame, guilt, and feelings of inadequacy. Some lies persist even in the face of facts to the contrary, others can never be exposed as untruths, and some are known as social conventions where it is feared that the truth would not be appreciated by the receiver, and so, to preserve cordiality, a lie is presented.

Uptight people who lie do so with a conviction that they are superior, entitled, and that others are inferior and deserve whatever the uptight person chooses to do. They are able to dismiss most challenges to their veracity, and can even turn a challenge around on the person who brought the lie to their attention. They can be adept at sidestepping the challenge by saying that the other person misunderstood what was said, is inaccurate in their reporting, has an ax to grind or a hidden agenda for the challenge, is trying to embarrass or shame the uptight person, and other such diversionary tactics. The challenger is then on the defensive and the focus is turned away from the lie. If, for some reason, the diversion does not work, the challenger can then become the target of the uptight person's vengeance for shaming him/her.

If you work, live, or are close to an uptight person of this type you can try the following coping strategies:

- Expect lies and don't become too upset when you get them over and over again.
- Be willing to expend some time and effort to verify what he/she tells you and not take everything they say at face value.
- Stay aware that they will be furious when challenged, and stand your ground if challenging the lie is important to you.
- You can consciously choose if the relationship and your personal integrity are important enough to ignore or overlook the lying behavior.

## COMPETITIVE

Competition can be invigorating and exciting, and provide a challenge to extend your efforts when it is constructive. Destructive competition, on the other hand, can produce immoral and unethical behavior, can become excessive where people are hurt, promote suspiciousness and contentiousness leading to impaired relationships, and other such negative consequences. It is the destructive aspects that conniving and manipulative uptight people seem to favor and use, and their use and need for rivalry seems to be unlimited.

Further, some of these people can be unscrupulous in the methods they use when competing. "All's fair" is their motto. When someone is willing to go all out to "win," it is difficult, if not impossible, to deter, prevent, or contain them. Terrorists provide a vivid example of this mind set. Just when you employ one barrier or constraint, they come at you from another direction putting you on edge and anxious almost all of the time.

These people are driven by the need to assure themselves that they are superior, and to ward off the emptiness with the self. Without the driving force and excitement that competition provides, they would be left to experience the emptiness with all the terror, despair, and depression felt when the emptiness is encountered.

Destructive competitiveness is hard to combat as you don't know what means they will use to "win;" you don't realize that they are almost always, if not always, in a competitive mode, and any trivial situation may arouse the competition. It is extremely difficult to be cooperative or collaborative with them as that would require some mutual trust, and you either cannot trust them, or don't know when or if to trust them. About the only strategies available to you are the following:

- If you must compete, do so fairly even when the other person is not.
- Opt out of competition with the uptight person whenever possible.
- Be alert to the negative signs and aspects of competition with the person and/or others.
- Live up to and maintain your morals, scruples, ethics, and principles.
- Encourage cooperation and collaboration for co-workers, friends, and family.

## VINDICTIVENESS

Spiteful and inclined to be vengeful are two descriptors for vindictive people. They retaliate for whatever they feel is against them, act in ways to inflict hurt and embarrassment on others for trivial reasons, and hold grudges so as to be able to continue their vengeance for a long time. Any insult or other offense is a debt owed to them that is never fully paid off, and they continue to exact payment in mean and spiteful ways long after the original offense. To get an idea of how this happens with some people who are not uptight, just think of all of the people who are in their forties and fifties who still smart about offenses that happened to them while in high school. This gives you some notion of just how widespread and long some people can carry their hurt. The uptight person carries all the hurt they have encountered in their lives, some real and some imagined. They will use every opportunity that emerges to act to "get even," including vengeful acts in subtle and little ways. Some examples of vindictiveness include the following:

- Arbitrarily and capriciously refusing or denying someone something that is important to them
- Exaggerating others' mistakes, flaws, and the like
- Passing on unfounded rumors and gossip that are detrimental to the person
- Subtle acts and attitudes of hostility
- Using their power position in inappropriate ways against the person, such as chastising them in public; being dismissive of their thoughts, ideas, or feelings in the presence of others; and denigrating them whenever possible especially when others are present
- Acting against the person's spouse, partner, child, or other family member

Nothing you do or say will make a difference to the vindictive person, even if they appear to accept an apology or explanation. No amount of apologizing, trying to be reasonable, acting in friendly ways, or trying to appeal to their "better nature" will bring about any change in their vindictive behavior. They will continue to be spiteful in unexpected ways and at unexpected times.

Your greatest challenge will be to manage and contain your negative emotions, some of which can be intense at times, to not take into your self the criticism or blame that they dispense, and to maintain your positive self-esteem. Any attempts by you to confront or retaliate are likely to intensify the vengeful behavior, and/or to make bad matters worse. Limit contact with this person, don't give them ammunition to use against you, and don't try to enlist others on your side. The people you try to enlist may tell the uptight person, which will only intensify their vindictiveness.

## EXPLOITIVE

The self-absorption of the Conniving and Manipulative type causes them to be exploitive of others, and to feel that it is their right to do so. Others are expected to comply and to not protest the exploitation. To exploit others is to take advantage of them in some way for personal gain. Exploitation can happen as a result of a power differential, such as what occurs in sexual and other harassment; the ignorance of the exploited person, such as what can happen with con tricks; fears, such as feeling apprehension about people from another culture; and capitalizing on the other person's good nature, such as what can happen with people who are eager to please others. Exploitation can be physical, emotional, sexual, spiritual, relational, and so on. It can take place for just about every part of our being and in every part of our lives.

Exploitation by an uptight person can just be a part of who they are, and they act on this unconsciously much of the time. These people have an incomplete sense of where their self ends and where others' begin, making that boundary indistinct and unrecognizable. Thus, others are perceived as extensions of the self, and are under the uptight person's control to do with as they see fit. Some can view others as "marks" who exist to be taken, gypped, swindled, and so on. Most all of them will expect favors with little or no reciprocity, but they also feel free to solicit these favors somewhat frequently. Other people are perceived by them as being in an inferior position or of inferior status. These uptight people can be arrogant and contemptuous in their perceptions and behaviors with others.

If you are a trusting person, wanting to believe the best of others, and/or desirous of appreciation and approval from almost everyone, you can find that you are exploited more than you would like, although any exploitation is too much. Your openness, desire to believe in the best of others, and your socialized personality predisposes you to become a target of exploitation, and this can be especially so in the case where you are in an intimate or work relationship with the Conniving and Manipulative uptight person. These people can be adept at reading others and capitalizing on others' needs and vulnerabilities.

They seem to be able to sense when others are available for exploitation. You may not be able to prevent all exploitation of you, but you can moderate the amount, prevent some, and build your self so as to reduce the frequency of these, and the negative effects on you. Strategies include the following:

- Pay attention to your sense of a possible exploitive request, demand, or act. Take time to reflect before acquiescing or acting.
- Do favors only when you want to, and not because someone wants one, or is coercing you to do the favor.
- Don't look for favors to be returned, or ask for favors from the uptight person. Try and do for yourself as much as possible, but in the case of a real need, do ask for the favor, but from someone else.
- Try not to be exploited by the same person more than once. Learn from the experience.
- Practice acting in accord with your principles and values, and don't do things that would violate these, or that are destructive for you.

## CONTEMPTUOUS

Some attitudes and behaviors that can signal contempt are the following. Read these and determine if you have experienced four or more of these from the uptight person in your life.

| | |
|---|---|
| Disdain | Turn one's back upon |
| Scorn | Slight |
| Snub | Ignore |
| Rebuff | Disregard |
| Turn one's nose up toward | Overlook |
| Neglect | Give the cold shoulder to |

If you have experienced four or more of these from the uptight person in your life, you are probably carrying some feelings like resentment, anger, shame, feelings of inadequacy, and so on. Feeling someone's contempt of you can be infuriating, hurtful, and disappointing.

It may help to remember that contemptuous people need to consider others as inferior so that they can maintain a feeling of superiority, and to shore up their self-esteem. This means that you do not have to take the attitudes and behavior as personally directed toward you, but can think of these as that person's way to try and cope with conscious and unconscious doubts about self-worth, self-efficacy, and so on.

What are some strategies to use when you encounter contempt?

- Don't use contempt in return. You'll look more confident and in control if you return a put-down or other sign of contempt with courtesy and civility.
- Don't openly label what was done or said as contemptuous, especially in the presence of others, and don't mumble this under your breath. You may be fuming internally, but saying nothing may be your best choice at this point.
- Monitor your facial expression to keep it neutral and to not let your hurt, anger, or self-doubts be reflected by your expression.
- Don't buy into how the contemptuous person characterizes you. Use your self-affirmations that you will develop in a later chapter.
- Refrain from responding with something flattering or complimentary about the person directing contempt at you as he/she is likely to see that as his/her due, but it will not reduce or stop the contempt toward you.

Neutrality, social niceties such as courtesy and civility, and confidence in yourself are the most effective strategies.

## RUTHLESS

Indifference to others' rights and responsibilities, a lack of empathy, and extreme self-absorption characterize ruthless people. Of course, they never see themselves as ruthless, or without compassion or mercy, as they are cut off from these emotions, or they never developed these. It is important for you to know and accept this about the uptight person in your life when he/she displays these attitudes and behaviors. Other people simply do not exist for them as separate and worthwhile, they are barriers to what the uptight person wants, and barriers are not tolerated by them, they are eliminated by any means possible.

- Rules, regulations, and even laws are thought by them to be of little importance, barriers to be circumvented or ignored, and applicable only to others.

- "Paying dues," earning rewards, and the like are foreign concepts to these people and they feel that they are entitled to achieve without struggle, effort, or even expertise.
- They do not anticipate or feel the effects of their actions on other people, nor do they care about this.
- Intensity of focus and effort allow them to be successful at achieving their goals as they let nothing get in their way toward achieving these, including attending to personal relationships.
- Others are useful as pawns and dupes when their contributions are needed to get what is wanted. Once this is achieved, those who helped are dropped and discounted.

About the only strategy that will be helpful is to try to stay out of their way. If you are a boss or supervisor, you can insist that rules, regulations, and policies be followed and monitor this, but unless you are aware and diligent, they will find ways around these "inconveniences." Do not collaborate with them, as you will likely be left "holding the bag," wondering why and how you ended up in a fix or mess, left dangling without any acknowledgment or support from the person, and having to bear the consequences for his/her ruthless acts. If you were to benefit or get any rewards, you could be left with some guilt and shame for how these were achieved.

## ENVIOUS

The Controlling and Manipulative type can have excessive and extreme envy, and their desires to have what others have can propel them to do and say things to try and destroy others who have what they feel should be rightfully theirs, and are less deserving and capable. So, it's not just the desire for what the other person has, is, or does; that desire is accompanied by the notion that the other person is inferior and not worthy, and that the uptight person is superior, worthy, capable, and so on. Therefore, the other person needs to be shown that he/she is inferior and not deserving of whatever is envied. This mindset then allows the mean, spiteful, and underhanded acts that some uptight people use against the envied person.

How do you feel about people who have more money than you do, or those who have achieved more, or those with talents and competencies you lack but wish you had, or people who seem to have the kind of relationships you don't and for which you long, or the rich and famous that are in the national spotlight receiving considerable attention and admiration, or accomplished performers, athletes, and the like? Do you envy them? Do you wish you could change places with that person, as you could do or be better than they are? Let's consider situations in your current life, such as your workplace, school, or community. Are there one or more people in this setting that has something you want and feel you deserve, and that the other person does not warrant what is wanted by you? Maybe you think that the other person is favored by powerful people, or that your talents and contributions are being overlooked, ignored, or discounted, or that unfair practices led to the other person being favored. If any of these questions and statements resonates, you may be experiencing envy similar to that which uptight people feel, but it may not be as much or as intense. You may not act against the other person, whereas the uptight person is more likely to act against the envied person.

You cannot prevent acts arising from others' envy, nor do you have much protection against or from them. The envious person may not even have conscious awareness of his/her envy, and uses other explanations for his/her feelings, such as there was preferential treatment for that person, unfairness and/or injustice, the envious person is being discounted and/or minimized, the "fix" was in, and other such reasons or rationalizations. You also may not recognize that negative attitudes and acts are being fueled by envy, and may even discount the notion that you are envied. Failure to recognize envy leaves you open to confusion and hurt when the envy leads to acts against you; such as starting untrue negative rumors about you, tattling and telling lies to present you unfavorably, discounting and minimizing your accomplishments; refusing to consider your ideas and suggestions; excluding you from events, discussions, and the like, and making sarcastic and negative comments about and to you. About the only strategies you have at your command are to be aware when envy could be the reason for someone's negative attitudes and acts, to not let yourself be hurt by these to the point where your self-esteem is impacted, and to continue to be successful at whatever is envied.

## COERCIVE

Coercion is similar to bullying, but is more subtle. Bullying is more overt and there can be behaviors that can be observed and identified.

Coercion, on the other hand, operates more in the shadows, and can be difficult to pinpoint or observe. The goals for both bullying and for coercion are domination, power, and control. The person using coercion is out to subdue and defeat others, and to demonstrate their superiority. Coercive acts include the following:

- Implied threats with plausible deniability if confronted or challenged
- An air of smoldering anger that threatens to erupt and seems potentially dangerous
- Suggestions of possible generalized negative consequences for not complying, such as losing out on a raise or promotion
- Reminders of favors done for you, or other kinds of support that suggest reciprocity at this time
- Telling you that you are the only one taking this position, everyone else is in agreement with him/her
- Asking you why you aren't cooperating as this implies some obstruction on your part
- Suggesting that you are often "out of sync" with everyone else
- Saying and doing things intended to arouse your guilt or shame to get you to agree with what he/she wants from you
- Saying and doing things intended to arouse your guilt or shame to get you to comply

Notice that most coercion needs your cooperation in order to be effective. Your self-doubts about your adequacy, efficacy, and the like; your need to be liked and approved of; your fears about destruction, abandonment, and self-worth; your failure to establish and monitor your psychological boundaries; and other such personal factors can cause you to respond favorably to coercion. You can fear losing affection, your position, your dreams and ambitions, and other positives for you, and this predisposes you to react to the coercion and to do things you do not want to do, or that are destructive to your sense of your self, and/or your ethics, morals, and principles. You buy into the real or fantasy negative consequences that are implied.

Uptight people who use coercion have a need to dominate and control in order to feel adequate, and success at domination reinforces their feelings of superiority, of being unique and special, and of being entitled to continue to coerce others. Their self-absorption prohibits them from seeing and understanding the negative effects on others, and others tend to be intimidated and give in to keep the peace.

Strategies that can be helpful include the following:

- Refuse to act when coercion is being used, and act only when you freely choose to do so.
- Stand your ground and act in accord with your values, morals, ethics, and principles.
- Assess the threat and possible consequences before acting. For example, how likely is it that you will lose the affection of that person, and is it worth what you will have to give up about your self to get or keep this?
- Evaluate your need for harmony, affection, liking, and or approval, and judge the price you pay for what you receive in return.

## SEDUCTION

Like coercion, seduction is a subtle form of bullying, and uses your cooperation to exert power, dominance, and control. Your cooperation is solicited and fueled by your deepest desires and needs, your undeveloped narcissism, and your self-perceptions. Seducers use these to obtain what they want, and are very adept and successful at reading others accurately, and tapping in to their needs and desires to further the seducer's personal gain.

The act of seduction is to beguile, corrupt, entice, win over, and/or trick someone into doing something against their best interests, morals, ethics, or principles, and which may also be destructive for the person. This leaves the seducer in a winning position. Yes, the seduced person could have refrained or refused to participate, but he/she was blinded by the seducer from acting in his/her best interests.

The seduced person was blinded by one or more of the following personal factors:

- Greed and avarice
- The deep desire to be liked and approved of by almost everyone
- Attention seeking needs
- Admiration-hungry desires

- Lust
- Fear of loneliness, isolation, and/or alienation
- Wanting to be accepted and included
- Grandiosity and an entitlement attitude

When it comes to seduction, you can be your own worst enemy, and the uptight person uses this for his/her advantage. They suck you in by pretending that they think you are as wonderful as you think you are, and almost everyone responds favorably to this. This is another reason why some people continue to be seduced, and don't seem to learn no matter how frequent and hurtful the lesson is.

Self-knowledge and self-understanding can be of immense help to prevent becoming seduced. Accepting that you have one or more of the previously listed factors, and that these are influencing your susceptibility to seduction can lead you to developing your self so that you don't get misled into doing things you don't want to do, and for which you later feel regretful. Other than self-growth, you can practice asking the following questions before you act when it is possible that you are being seduced:

- Am I feeling any disquiet?
- Am I blinded by some of my needs and desires?
- Is the other person genuine in telling me what I want to hear?
- Do I want to hear this and/or want his/her approval so much that I'm willing to compromise who I am, and my values?

The answers to these may help you re-think what you were about to do.

# 8

# "Everyone and Everything Is Against Me": The Revengeful Complainer Type

Some uptight people seem to display their grandiosity more than they do its flipside, the impoverished self, and others exhibit the reverse. This type, the Revengeful Complainer, presents to others the impoverished, poor-me self most often, concealing the grandiosity that lurks ever near. This can be one reason why it is so difficult to communicate and relate with this type as most people tend to respond to what is exhibited. However, if you don't recognize that the underlying grandiosity is so close and can be mobilized in a nanosecond, you can often be puzzled, confused, and frustrated in interactions with this type of person. In addition, this type can be so hypersensitive to anything that could possibly carry a smidgen of criticism or blame that they tend to see these at every turn, and exact vengeance for the perceived attack on their self.

Their inner worlds are dismal, lacking enjoyment, and full of imagined terrors waiting to engulf them at any moment. They have to be hypervigilant to ward off engulfment and, at the same time, they have to keep defenses mounted against attacks from the outside world and its real and imagined terrors. They are trapped between the two, experiencing little or no respite. The constant tension and stress contribute to physical, cognitive, emotional, and relational concerns and problems. To gain a clearer idea of the negative attitudes and behaviors for this type, complete the following exercise.

**Exercise 8.1**

**Revengeful and Complaining**

*Materials*: A copy of the following form, one or more sheets of paper, and a pen or pencil

*Directions*: Use the following rating scale to rate the uptight person in your life:

5–Always or almost always; extremely like him/her
4–Very often; very much like him/her
3–Frequently; somewhat like him/her
2–Seldom; a little like him/her
1–Never or almost never; nothing like him/her

| | |
|---|---|
| 1. Perceives attacking behavior from almost everyone | 5 4 3 2 1 |
| 2. Others generally fail to meet his/her exacting standards | 5 4 3 2 1 |
| 3. Can find something that is wrong, needs fixing or correcting for just about everything | 5 4 3 2 1 |
| 4. When things don't go as planned, the person becomes very frustrated and is irritable and cranky | 5 4 3 2 1 |
| 5. Conversations seem to focus on or include his/her complaints | 5 4 3 2 1 |
| 6. Feels treated unfairly or unjustly | 5 4 3 2 1 |
| 7. Tends to focus on minor and trivial details to show how something or someone is not "right" or perfect | 5 4 3 2 1 |
| 8. Cannot accept anything as being "good enough" | 5 4 3 2 1 |
| 9. Makes cutting remarks to and about others | 5 4 3 2 1 |
| 10. Is sarcastic | 5 4 3 2 1 |
| 11. Seems to grudgingly give approval, affection, and the like | 5 4 3 2 1 |
| 12. Has withheld approval, affection, and/or resources to get even with someone | 5 4 3 2 1 |

13. Attempts to humiliate and/or embarrass
others

5 4 3 2 1

14. Uses put-downs and other demeaning
comments

5 4 3 2 1

15. His/her comments contain words like
should and ought to describe what he/she
perceives as right or good

5 4 3 2 1

Scoring: Add up ratings to derive a total score

64–75 Tends to be extremely revengeful and complaining
52–63 Tends to very revengeful and complaining
40–51 Tends to be frequently revengeful and complaining
28–39 Tends to be somewhat revengeful and complaining
15–27 Can be revengeful and complaining at times

2. Review the items rated 4 and 5, and list each on a sheet of paper, leaving some writing space between each listed item.

3. Take the listed items one at a time and list your observations and feelings about the attitude or behavior. Also note any actions you've taken to try and modify or change the attitude or behavior.

4. Review what you wrote and write a summary paragraph about the effects (your feelings) of the revengeful complaining attitudes and behaviors, and your feelings about your success at getting the person to modify or change any of these.

5. Reflect on what you wrote and write one strategy you can employ to prevent one or more feelings that arise from your responses to the person's behavior. Examples for possible strategies include the following:

- Say nothing
- Give up saying or doing things to try and get them to change
- Leave their presence
- Stop trying to make him/her feel better when things don't go as planned
- Don't respond to sarcasm, cutting remarks, and the like

You can create your own strategies, and I strongly suggest that you create some constructive ones. Let's examine the attitudes and behaviors, and propose additional strategies.

## PERCEIVED ATTACKS

By now you probably understand that the inner experiencing of this type predisposes them to be constantly on guard against real or imagined hostile attacks. This predisposition causes them to view what others say and do as personally directed toward them, and that these are attempts to hurt and destroy their self. Their goal is the protection of the self at all costs.

This unconscious attitude can cause them to also use attacks as preemptive defensive strikes, and to respond in inappropriate ways because they are expecting or seeing attacks where none exist. Preemptive strikes are to keep others off balance, edgy, wary, and cautious, and this can work. Others don't know if other attacks are on the way, or if they have unintentionally offended, or even if they (the receiver) have misread the attacker's intent. Examples of preemptive strikes can include the following:

- Using a challenging manner to ask "why" or "what" questions about what the person did, did not do, or even about their thoughts
- "Jumping down someone's throat," especially when this is unexpected, or for no discernable reason at the time
- Deliberately putting someone on the defensive
- Challenging someone before even acknowledging social niceties, e.g., greeting the person

Preemptive strikes can be very effective, and can be hard to prevent. A usual response from the receiver is to become defensive by explaining, soothing the attacker, or apologizing without understanding why an apology seems to be called for. The receiver is left with intense negative feelings, mostly about him/herself. Some receivers may return the attack, which likely leads to a conflict and more negative intense feelings. Strategies that could be more effective include the following:

- Don't answer right away. Instead, institute courtesy and civility as a response prior to any other response. For example, greet the person and ask how he/she is feeling. This gives you time to manage and contain your feelings, highlights their lack of courtesy and civility, and lowers the intensity level.

- Respond to their underlying feelings instead of responding to the content. Ask something like, " Is something upsetting you?"
- Refuse to become defensive, and explain only when it is requested *and* if you feel an explanation is warranted. Otherwise, address another topic.

When the revengeful complainer uses attacks as inappropriate responses, these can be strong defenses to deflect attention away from them, and cause others to turn their attention to a counter defense. Examples for attacks as inappropriate responses are as follows:

- Bringing up old grievances, offenses, and the like
- Pointing out the other person's perceived weaknesses, lapses, inadequacies, and so on, especially when these (even if they are accurate) would have nothing to do with the current conversation
- Making a joke about the person, his/her delivery of information, appearance, or other ways of poking fun to put the other person at a disadvantage or in a poor light
- Responding with sarcasm
- Devaluing the person and/or what was said or done

When inappropriate responses are given, the most effective strategies are to leave, to ignore them when possible, and to act as if there was no attack. Other kinds of responses are likely to escalate the hostilities.

## EXACTING STANDARDS

Have you ever experienced something similar to the following? You had worked hard to try and take care of every detail and to anticipate any potential problems for an event, like a family dinner; or a project, such as a report at work. You wanted it to be as perfect as possible understanding that anything could intervene to thwart your plans, or that you may not have anticipated everything. The event occurs or the project is complete, and now the uptight person is present and involved. He/she immediately zooms in on a minor imperfection, and points it out to you, noting something that directly says, or indirectly infers, that you can never get it right and that you are inadequate.

If you have experienced the fallout from the Revengeful Complainer type's exacting standards, you probably know what fury and humiliation feel like. In spite of all of the positives, they seem to be able to only see the negatives, or less than what they consider to be perfection. This attitude extends to other people, and it doesn't seem to matter to them that others care for them, try to please them, or work to meet their exacting standards. All the uptight people see is that the other person failed to meet his/her standards. What you may not realize if you are on the receiving end of their displeasure, is that they too do not meet these impossible standards, and this failure is very painful for them. Even though they can hide their failures from others, they see and remember them. One of their responses for their failures is to off-load the responsibility for these failures onto someone else. Another response is to deflect attention to how you and/or others are inadequate.

Embedded in this attitude of having to have perfection for just about everything or for everything, is the inner fear that disorder, imperfection, or flaws will mean that his/herself will be destroyed. The anxiety about the preservation of the self is acute and continual. The external world must be in order as that person perceives it so that their internal disorder and fears can be mollified, managed, and contained. Any imperfection in the person's exacting standards can signal chaos and destruction of the self, and others as extensions of the person are expected to know and understand this, and to always ensure that no threat to their self occurs, such as what can happen when the standards are not met.

Trying to meet these deep seated and likely unconscious needs and demands is futile. Neither you nor the uptight person will be able to fully meet these all of the time, or even most of the time. It can be commendable to work for perfection, but is also an unrealistic expectation, and you have to decide how much of your time and energy you are willing to devote to the impossible task. You can decide to do your best, and that good enough is acceptable sometimes, or you can feel compelled to continue on the futile quest for perfection and always trying to please the uptight person.

## NOT AS PLANNED

This type can plan to the extent that they try to micromanage every detail, and their anxiety, intensity, and self-absorption makes them difficult and uncomfortable to be around or to work with when they are executing whatever they planned. These people become easily frustrated, displace their frustration and blame onto others, project their displeasure onto others when things do not happen as they wanted or planned, and can easily criticize others. Their inner chaos comes to the forefront to encourage these negative behaviors. Worse can be when they have to participate in carrying out or participating in what others planned. Their exacting standards increase their inclinations to be dissatisfied, to find fault, and to nitpick.

Not only must their plans be carried out, they can also have an unrealistic expectation that the plans are so perfect that everything and everyone will fall into line and place without exception. There will be no delays, glitches, problems, or the like because the universe is under their control. Thus, the slightest deviation, whether trivial or large, sends them into a tizzy and they are then prone to overreact.

The Revengeful Complainer type can complain and whine a lot about how things never seem to go as planned, and that nothing is done right, except by them of course. They can openly say or imply that the world would be a better place if more people were like them. They have the grandiosity and arrogance, as well as the impoverished ego state, operating at almost the same time.

Trying to soothe them by being logical and reasonable does not work even if they seem to agree, because their inner states are demanding that the outer world be orderly, controlled by them, and that it complies with what they want or plan, and so on. You are likely to find yourself in the position of being blamed and criticized for not doing enough to ensure that things are done "right," or will go as planned. You can be blamed even when the problems and/or glitches are unavoidable and not under your control. The unfairness and unreasonableness of their attitudes and charges are what produces your frustration, hurt, or anger. Instead of trying to meet their unrealistic expectations or responding to their unfounded charges, you will find it more rewarding and constructive to learn to control, manage, and contain your feelings. Techniques for dealing with your feelings are presented in later chapters.

## DETAIL ORIENTED

Being detail oriented can be a positive characteristic when it is not excessive. But, in the case with this type, their detail orientation is over the top. These are the people who are attuned to the trivial, minute, and insignificant details that do not make much or any difference to the outcomes, functioning, or acceptability of whatever they are connected to. They can fuss, fret, and obsess over things that don't amount to anything, irritate others with their constant complaining and demands about the trivial details, and spend considerable time, energy, and resources trying to take care of every detail.

There are situations and circumstances where you do want attention given to details, such as surgery, maintenance of vehicles like automobiles and airplanes, filling prescriptions, and safety features of gadgets as these can have serious repercussions for lives. These are not what we're talking about here. This discussion is about excessive and obsessive attention to details such as how the dishes should or must be placed in the dishwasher, how to squeeze the toothpaste from the tube, finding specks of dust that no one else can see, and everything—and I do mean everything—must be perfectly aligned. It's not so much that the uptight person needs this order and control, it's more that they demand that others buy into and comply with their excessive needs and perceptions of how things should or ought to be. Not only are others expected to perceive the world and needs as they do, others must prevent the frustrations that arise when details are not attended to in the necessary (to them) way. What is most troubling to the uptight person's relationships is that they nag, fuss, carp, complain, and berate others who don't seem to attend to or care about the "right" way or excessive details, and they never give up.

Others have few effective strategies to use in these circumstances. They are limited to giving in and complying, or doing what they can and not sweating the small stuff, or becoming indifferent and ignoring the uptight person's expectations and demands. Whatever the relationship is with the uptight person, the other person in the relationship has to weigh the pros and cons of the chosen strategy.

## LOUDLY COMPLAINS

The Revengeful Complainer uptight person does not suffer in silence. These people complain often and loudly to ensure that all within hearing distance are aware of their suffering, and find reasons to complain for just about everything. They tell details about their complaints, seem to never forget about these, and can continue to re-hash them off and on even for years. Some may whine, some recount their complaints with an air of barely tolerated suffering, and some seem to begin many statements with, "I don't mean (or want) to complain, but. . ."

These complaints are their attempts to accomplish the following:

- Get the external world to order things so that their internal anxious world will be soothed and pacified
- To manipulate and control others to do what they want them to do
- As a demonstration of their helplessness and ineffectiveness so that others will rescue them and they will not have to take responsibility for their own welfare
- To show how courageous and brave they are to bear so much suffering
- To satisfy their attention-hungry and/or admiration-seeking needs
- As a way to blame and criticize others

Others who must interact with them on a regular basis can try to stem the complaints by taking care of some of the problems, or by ignoring these, or by trying to focus their attention on some positives, or by being sympathetic. However, none of these strategies do anything to reduce or eliminate their constant complaining. New problems take the place of those that others helped resolve; the uptight person challenges attempts to ignore these and labels the other person as unfeeling and uncaring, can become angry at attempts to deflect their complaints, and can be a bottomless pit at needing sympathy.

Semi-effective strategies can include the following:

- Accept that nothing you do or say will reduce or eliminate their complaints.
- Make neutral comments that convey your understanding of the suffering or validity of the complaints, but take no action except when acting is your responsibility.
- If or when it's warranted, compliment him/her on bearing up so well under the circumstances.
- Refrain from pointing out that the person complains a lot, as this could be enraging to him/her.

## FAILS TO ASSUME RESPONSIBILITY

This type is not the only type of person who fails to take responsibility for their feelings, growth, and development, but they do have this characteristic almost universally. Whatever is not perfect, or when there are mistakes or errors, or when things don't go as they had planned, they can rearrange their thoughts so that they don't have to assume responsibility and be faulted. The failure to take responsibility is to prevent being shamed for what they perceive as fatal flaws for the self. They cannot bear to even consider that they have flaws, and/or that others can see these flaws, for fear that they will be abandoned or destroyed. This is a deep-seated pervasive fear of long standing that can be associated as the basis for many of their self-absorbed and troubling behaviors and attitudes that negatively impact their relationships.

Even when or if the Revengeful Complainer seems to accept responsibility at first, subsequent statements and comments will negate this acceptance. Excuses, rationalizations, and off-loading blame onto another person are some ways that the original statement is negated. Frequently expressed are suspicions about others' motives for noticing what happened, such as the person "having it in" for the uptight person, and deflection to how others are inadequate. In their minds they are blameless, and at the mercy of malicious other people, and they must preserve the perception of the blameless self at all costs and by any means possible.

This scenario is played out even when assumption of responsibility would not be a big deal, or carries little or no negative consequences. Their grandiosity and omnipotence do not permit their being able to perceive their self as less than perfect, and any assumption of responsibility for a mistake, no matter how trivial, would mar the perfection; that simply must not happen. Their self is perfect, and external forces are always trying to mar the perfection.

There are no strategies that can help you or anyone reach this uptight person to get them to assume any portion of the responsibility. In addition, because of their inclination toward revenge, they will become angry at the attempts to get them to assume responsibility, and find ways to turn it back on the other person. Further, they can carry grudges about this, and exact their revenge for the perceived insult to their self over and over again. Others are being unfair to them and must be stopped and punished.

## SARCASM

Sarcasm is an indirect way of expressing displeasure, disapproval, and other negative feelings. It can also be used for revenge, to attack the other person and make them appear foolish, ignorant, stupid, or inadequate. It is used to humiliate and shame the person. At the same time, its intent is to cause the speaker to appear superior. Sarcasm is one way to show contempt for another person.

Uptight people of the Revengeful Complainer type can effectively use sarcasm as one of their tools to exact vengeance on others they perceive as threats, as inferior to them, or as in need of punishment, or as a reminder of just who is superior. It is used so that the uptight person does not have to assume any responsibility for its negative impact, inferences, or connotations. If challenged about the remark, they can deny any negative intent, and put the receiver on the defensive when they suggest that the receiver does not understand, or is unable to see the disguised humor. "I was just being sarcastic (or joking)," can be the uptight person's response to a challenge.

Embedded in sarcasm are thinly masked feelings that are too dangerous for the person to openly express. Sarcasm can carry some of the following messages of how the speaker feels about the target and receiver of the remarks:

- I don't like you.
- I feel you are inadequate, ineffective, and shameful.
- You should be more like me and then you wouldn't be ignorant or make mistakes.
- You are too (dangerous, stupid, inept, etc.) for me to directly express my feelings.
- I'm superior to you in every way.

Effective strategies when you are the target of sarcasm are to ignore the nastiness underlying the remark and respond seriously to the content, or not respond at all; change the subject to something more positive; and when appropriate or feasible, just leave the sarcastic person's presence. If the speaker is an uptight person, especially one of this type, do not challenge the content, tone, or intent of the sarcastic remark.

## CUTTING REMARKS, PUT-DOWNS, ETC.

While sarcasm is an indirect expression of contempt, cutting remarks and put-downs are direct ways to express contempt, and to imply that the person is inferior. These remarks that devalue the receiver are intended to hurt, to influence others' perceptions of the receiver in a negative way, and to emphasize the speaker's superiority. Revengeful Complainer uptight people exact their revenge and show their hostility in this way even when they like to believe that they are "just being honest."

These kinds of direct negative expressions can lose much of their power to hurt and shame when the receiver of these does not react to them, or buy into the depreciating intent. Not reacting, especially in the presence of the speaker, takes away his/her pleasure and deflates some of the arrogance. They've given you a shot that should wound, but it doesn't appear to have accomplished its goal. To not react requires some prior preparation on the receiver's part, such as anticipating the remarks because of prior experiences, or using the emotional insulation described in chapter 9, or instituting the strategies described below. The immediate goal is to not give the uptight person the satisfaction of knowing that the remarks or put-downs found their target and wounded you. Try using one or more of the following strategies:

- Be, or pretend to be, indifferent.
- Use your cognitive self-talk to support yourself, such as saying to yourself, "I don't have to, or I will not, show my real reaction."
- Shrug your shoulders to convey indifference.
- Make a neutral remark, and change the subject.

It is important that the receiver does not buy into the cutting remark or put-down, and react defensively by explaining, protesting, or mounting a counterattack. These are seldom effective as they reinforce the validity of the remarks, and give the uptight person reinforcement that he/she was indeed correct. Try to not identify with any part of the put-down or cutting remark. This means that even if you think or fear that some part of what was said was accurate about you, it is rejected for the moment. You can explore this later if you choose. However, while in the presence of the uptight person, you need to convince yourself that what was said is not reflective of you in any way. Other strategies can include building up your self-confidence over time, and having self-assurance that the negative comments are more about the other person than they are about you.

## ATTEMPTS TO HUMILIATE AND SHAME

Sarcasm, put-downs, cutting remarks, and the like are some of the attempts to shame and humiliate others that are used by uptight people, especially the Revengeful Complainer type. When these people can keep others from seeing the uptight person's real self (which he/she fears is flawed and shameful and, if seen, would lead to abandonment and/or destruction), he/she feels safer. Their goal is to preserve their self, and attacking others is one means for achieving that goal. Think about it; when you are attacked, you move to a defensive position where you are protecting your self, and are not trying to see or understand the attacker as he/she really is. Thus, they are accomplishing their goal with this tactic. Some strategies these people use to trigger others' shame, and or to humiliate them in the presence of others include the following:

- Using intimidating and bullying behavior
- Taunting
- Jeering at others or what they try to do
- Telling stories about the person's mistakes, ineptness, and so on
- Pointing out and/or emphasizing something negative or "not right" about the person
- Asking double bind questions where any answer would put the receiver in a poor light
- Constantly bringing up old instances where the person did not perform well, or made mistakes

These attempts to invoke shame and/or to humiliate the person in the presence of others can work very well, especially when the receiver is a thoughtful, reflective, and accepting of self kind of person who is aware of his/her imperfections. However, you don't have to let the uptight person know that he/she hit the target. Refuse to be bullied or intimidated, (See Chapter 7 for some suggestions on how to do this), don't respond to taunts or jeers; leave when they start to tell stories or say that you think that the present is more important than the past; be or pretend to be indifferent; engage your emotional insulation (see chapter 9) ; and focus on preventing the person from achieving his/her goal of invoking shame and humiliation for you. Denying their goal is the best strategy.

But it can also be important for you to not mount a counteroffensive; not to use the same tactics he/she is using, such as taunting, jeering, or bullying; using sarcasm or put-downs for him/her; or similar responses that are intended to hurt the other person. It can also be futile to challenge him/her, as that only intensifies and escalates what they are doing, or to show in any way that you are hurt by these attempts to shame and humiliate, as the uptight person is indifferent to your feelings, and lacks empathy.

## WITHHOLDS APPROVAL, AFFECTION

If withholding anything causes hurt and distress for another person, then the Revengeful Complainer uptight person will use this as a weapon. It's not that they forget to show these emotions as some other people do, or do not recognize their importance for the other person, it's that they deliberately set out to hurt that person, and their intent is difficult to identify or to challenge. Intentional withholding is sneaky, underhanded, and vicious.

Assume that the other person wanting the uptight person's approval and/or affection is an adult and not an adolescent or child whose self-development is nourished by approval and affection. An adult is assumed to have sufficient development of their self where approval and/or affection is appreciated and cherished, but their sense of self and self-worth are not dependent on receiving these from a particular person. They want approval and/or affection, but do not expect these from just anyone or almost everybody. However, some adults do not have sufficient self-development and can be dependent on others to supply these in order for them to have a sense of self-worth and self-esteem. These are the people who can be hurt and distressed when the uptight person withholds these. They will then work harder to gain the approval and/or affection from the uptight person, who then reinforces this need and behavior by intermittently providing and withholding these. The person is being manipulated by his/her needs and lack of self-development. Don't think for a moment that the uptight person is unaware of the person's needs and of the manipulation they are carrying out.

You cannot get the approval or affection you seek from this type. While the Spartan and Withholding type is also resistant to giving approval and affection among other things, they will do so under certain circumstances, and it is possible to obtain some measure of these from them. However, the Revengeful Complainer is using withholding to deliberately hurt the other person, and the more the person tries to get these from him/her, the greater pleasure and satisfaction he/she experiences. He/she may grudgingly give some approval or affection on occasion when the other person has sufficiently abased him/herself, but makes sure to let that person know that giving this is only or mostly because the person is so needy. You may get what you want, but you pay a considerable price, and the prize or reward is tarnished.

## SHOULD AND OUGHT

Rigid and unyielding ways of perceiving the world, and a deeply held conviction that they are right leads uptight people to use and imply should and ought in their interactions with others. They can be quick to point out to others what they (the other person) should and ought to be, do, think, feel, and so on. Sometimes this is directly expressed, while at other times the "should" and "ought" are strongly implied. They are also quick to inform others that they would not make mistakes, suffer consequences, and the like if they did what they should or ought to have done. Worse can be when the uptight person told you what you should or ought to do, you did not do what was suggested, and what you did, did not work out. This situation gives them an opportunity to gloat, feel superior, and reinforces their contempt for you. It would not be unusual to hear them say that things would have worked out if you had followed their guidance.

One of the reasons why nothing you do or say will promote change for the uptight person is their deeply held conviction that their perspective is the only "right" one, and they can give you many examples that support their perspective. They are closed to even a hint that they could be wrong. You go up against a formidable wall when you attack this conviction, and doing so even mildly can infuriate them and trigger their desire for revenge. It is difficult for most people to accept that someone is that rigid and unyielding, and so they make the mistake of trying to reason with the uptight person, present logical arguments, appeal to their non-existent empathy, or show disapproval of their perspective and conviction. Any of these actions can and do bring retaliation.

Are there strategies that can help you cope with this type when they are using should and ought and it is directed at you? Some of the following suggestions may provide you with ideas for creating your own strategies:

- Listen to what they have to say and ignore the should or ought as a dictate or demand. Embedded may be some useful information.
- Forgive yourself when things don't work out or you make a mistake. You can do better next time.
- Don't react visibly to "I told you so" or "If you had." Maybe it would have worked, but maybe it would not have worked.
- Don't ask the uptight person for guidance, suggestions, counsel, and the like, as they would expect you to adopt these without modification or questions.
- Accept that they have the conviction and perspective, and that you cannot change them.
- Refrain from challenging their perspective, conviction, or should and ought.

# 9

# Why They Get Next to You: Understand Your Reactions

This chapter focuses on you and your reactions to the uptight person in your life with whom you interact on a regular basis. This relationship has an importance in your life, and it is assumed that you either want or intend to keep the relationship out of choice or necessity, such as with a work-related relationship. Therefore, this chapter focuses on your desires and wishes for your relationships in general, triggered feelings in interactions with the uptight person, your characteristic relating style, the roles of old parental messages, your undeveloped narcissism, psychological boundaries, and an assessment of your current state of well-being. The next chapter presents additional coping strategies that build on your understanding of why you have the reactions that you have.

Let's begin with identifying your wishes and desires for your relationships. The level and kind for these will differ for the kind of relationship, for example, intimate versus work-related, or worker versus the boss. However, your basic wishes and desires will essentially remain the same.

**Exercise 9.1**

**Relationship Wishes and Desires**

*Materials*: A copy of the following scales, paper, a pen or pencil for writing, and a colored marker or pencil

*Directions*: Rate the importance of each item for you in a positive relationship

5–Absolutely essential
4–Extremely important
3–Very important
2–Somewhat important
1–Not important

| | | | | | |
|---|---|---|---|---|---|
| 1. Reciprocity of actions, feelings, and the like | 5 | 4 | 3 | 2 | 1 |
| 2. Mutual encouragement and support | 5 | 4 | 3 | 2 | 1 |
| 3. Acceptance of you as you are | 5 | 4 | 3 | 2 | 1 |
| 4. Expressions of warmth and caring | 5 | 4 | 3 | 2 | 1 |
| 5. Understanding | 5 | 4 | 3 | 2 | 1 |
| 6. Empathic responding | 5 | 4 | 3 | 2 | 1 |
| 7. Interest in you, attention to you | 5 | 4 | 3 | 2 | 1 |
| 8. Respect for you as a worthwhile unique person | 5 | 4 | 3 | 2 | 1 |
| 9. Genuineness of feelings toward you, and responses to you | 5 | 4 | 3 | 2 | 1 |
| 10. Trust | 5 | 4 | 3 | 2 | 1 |

Add your ratings to derive a total score. Then list two to five relationship wishes and desires you have that are not on the scale, and then rate these using the same scale. Next, review your ratings for items 1–10, and use the colored marker or pencil to check the extent or degree to which an item is present for the uptight person in your life. Then use the following scale to rate the extent or degree to which it exists in the relationship:

5–Always or almost always exhibited by that person
4–Frequently exhibited by that person
3–Exhibited on occasion
2–Seldom exhibited
1–Never or almost never exhibited

After rating each item, add your ratings to derive a total score. Then write the total scores for #2 and #4 side by side. These scores represent your wishes and desires versus the reality of how well or little these are met in the current relationship with an uptight person. If the discrepancy score is 35 or higher, there can be a considerable difference between what you want and expect in a relationship and the reality of what you are getting in the relationship you chose to rate. A low discrepancy score can indicate some congruence between what you want and what you receive in the rated relationship.

If you chose to rate a relationship where you cannot or choose to not leave, such as a workplace relationship, the discrepancy may be causing you considerable distress. You feel stuck, can feel helpless or hopeless, and can wonder why you cannot seem to make the relationship more positive and satisfying. You may not have realized that there was such a wide gap between your wishes and desires and the reality of the relationship, and this unawareness can also be contributing to your distress. It could also be helpful for you to reflect on your other relationships and see if some discrepancies also exist for these.

Information from completing the exercise could have established one point about your reactions to the uptight person, that is, you are not experiencing enough of your relationship wishes and desires with this person. One caveat—it is not known if any of your wishes and desires could be termed as extreme. The assumption is that your relationship wishes and desires are reasonable and logical for anyone.

## TRIGGERED FEELINGS

Uptight people seem to have a knack for triggering the intense feelings for others. While they do not make or cause others to have the feeling(s), they are able to do the following:

- Promote catching, incorporating, and acting out negative feelings
- Doing and saying things that are calculated to arouse feelings like anger that have their roots and associations with others' unresolved family of origin issues and other past experiences
- Tapping conscious or unconscious negative perceptions another has about him/herself, such as doubts about self-efficacy

There are numerous and unique reasons for your reactions that cannot be addressed here. What can be presented are some basic assumptions about your triggered feelings that, when accepted by you, can produce perceptual shifts to allow you to better manage and contain intense triggered feelings, and/or to reduce their intensity and impact on you. Also presented are a description of a usual response sequence, and a procedure for modifying the sequence to become more self-reflective and to modify your reactions. Prevention of catching projected feelings is discussed in the section on psychological boundaries, the unresolved issues and unfinished business relationship to triggered feelings are discussed in the section on old parental messages, and tapping one's conscious or unconscious self-thoughts is discussed in the section on undeveloped narcissism.

## Basic Assumptions and Needed Perceptual Shifts

1. Your feelings are under your control and are not "caused" by others. Shift to accepting that you choose your feelings, and your reactions can be the outcome from other associations, such as transference.
2. Other people are not responsible for your thoughts and feelings, particularly those thoughts and feelings about your self. Shift to perceiving that you can take responsibility for your feelings and for your self-development.
3. Aroused or triggered feelings are usually about you, how you perceive and feel about your self. Shift to examining these, becoming self-reflective and understanding that you can grow and develop positive perceptions and feelings.
4. Unresolved family of origin issues and other unfinished business get projected onto others and other relationships in disguised form; until these are resolved, you will continue to have intense and negative reactions to some comments and remarks. Shift to understanding that these need work to resolve so that you can be better fortified against their undue influences. This work may be facilitated with the assistance of a competent mental health professional.

## Usual Response Sequence

1. One or more feelings are aroused and identified, such as one or more of the following:
   - Fear—danger of destruction
   - Anger—fight or flight
   - Guilt—not living up to personal values, standards, etc.
   - Shame—being fatally flawed
2. Action is taken. One or more of the following are usual actions:
   - Fight—become hostile, attack

- Flight—withdraw physically or emotionally (example, sulking)
- Repression—pushed into the unconscious
- Denial—also pushed into the unconscious
- Minimization—downplaying its negative effects or impact
- Discounting—rationalizing that it wasn't hurtful, or wasn't meant
- Ignoring—pretending that it did not happen

3. The initial feeling becomes one or more of the following:
   - Modified or adapted
   - Stuffed
   - Smolders
   - Intensifies

The usual response sequence leaves you with uncomfortable residual feelings. The following self-reflective and self-exploration response will help modify and eliminate these uncomfortable feelings when substituted for the usual response. The described process is also helpful in containing and managing distressful feelings when they do arise.

## Self-reflective and Self-exploration Response

### Exercise 9.2 Changing The Usual Response Sequence

Directions: Find a quiet place to work on the process, one where you will not be disturbed. Slowly read through the questions and try to answer each.

1. Begin with identifying one or more feelings are aroused as in #1 above. Think of an event that aroused feelings such as anger, fear, shame, or guilt. Reflect on the event and answer the following questions.
2. Question to oneself—What do I think the event (what was said and/or done) is saying about me as a person? For example, could I be hearing or feeling one or more of the following?
   - I'm not good enough.
   - I am shameful and fatally flawed.
   - I'm not important and worthwhile, or of little consequence.
   - I will be abandoned (not liked, not approved of, and/or excluded).
   - I will be destroyed (failure to survive).
   - I'm not loveable.

3. Question to oneself—How true and/or valid is my thought about the comment (Your selection for #2)? Rate the truth/validity from 0 (none) to 10 (extremely true and valid).

4. Question to oneself—What evidence do I have that refute the negative thought? List specifics and then respond to the following:
   - How am I good enough—what do I do well?
   - How have I worked to reduce shameful feelings and/or actions that produce my shame? Do I act in accord with what I know and believe is "a good person"?
   - I am worthwhile, capable, and am important to people who love me (give names).
   - If I am abandoned at this time, I can form other connections and relationships.
   - Any destruction of me will be only happen because I let it happen, and I am resilient and hardy enough to survive.
   - I am loveable and I have one or more people that love me.

5. Question to oneself—What unresolved family of origin issues or other unfinished business could my reaction be associated with, e.g., transference or projection? If so, I may not be reacting to objective reality, but to associations from my past. Since the present is different, I can choose to feel differently.

6. Questions to oneself—Could all or part of my reaction be projective identification, or emotional contagion? If so, why did I incorporate the feelings of someone else, identify with them, and then act on these which are acts against my self? Is this also related to my unresolved family of origin issues or unfinished business? If so, what do I need to work on?
   - Am I getting in touch with deep and enduring pain/narcissistic injury?
   - Am I disappointed with my self, and thus am reacting to what appears to make visible my flaws and imperfections?
   - If any or all of this is accurate, I can help myself by working to resolve unresolved issues and unfinished business so that I do not react in a way that increases or promotes my distress.

## RELATING STYLES

Your personality interacting with your experiences in your family of origin, and those from past experiences, is the basis for your relating style. People relate to others in various ways depending on the relationship and the circumstances, and your style could be part of the reason for your reactions to the uptight person in your life. Following are some relating styles and a short description of some behaviors that can be typical for each style:

- Cognitive—Tends to think and analyze. Can be so caught up in thoughts that feelings are missed
- Needy—Tends to be clingy, demanding of attention and approval, but can never get enough of these
- Manipulative—Tends to use conscious and unconscious means to get others to give what is wanted
- Isolated—Tends to keep others at a distance, and resists attempts at intimacy or inclusion
- Self-absorbed—Tends to be more focused on his/her needs than those for others, also discounts or misses others' feelings
- Self-sacrificing—Tends to focus more on taking care of others and fulfilling their demands, and can neglect one's own self
- Charming—Tends to relate to others in ways that demonstrate warmth, caring, and positive regard, may not always be genuine
- Charismatic—Tends to relate in ways that meet others' needs, longing, wishes, and desires; can be used to manipulate others into self-destructive acts

The uptight person is intense, anxious, and self-absorbed, and is not overly concerned about others' feelings and reactions. Indeed, they tend to be indifferent to what is triggered or aroused in others by their attitudes and behaviors. These people seem to understand, consciously and unconsciously, how to use your relating style to help cause you the most discomfort. Following are samples of how your relating style can be used to promote certain uncomfortable reactions for you. While you can feel some form of fear, anger, guilt, and shame for all of these, one will tend to be most prominent.

Many people do not fit neatly into a category, and can exhibit a combination of styles, especially combining effective and ineffective styles. However, interactions with uptight people can trigger unpleasant feelings regardless of your preferred style. The task is to begin with awareness, integrate some understanding of your style and reactions, and to develop your self so as to moderate the effect of uptight people's attitudes and behaviors on you. Possible modifications relative to characteristic relating styles are as follows:

| Relating Style | Uptight Person's Actions | Your Reaction |
|---|---|---|
| Cognitive | Emphasizes feelings | Guilt, shame |
| Needy | Withholds approval, affection | Hurt, inadequacy |
| Manipulative | Attacks, points out flaws | Guilt |
| Isolated | Ignores, is dimissive | Anger |
| Self-absorbed | Attacks | Fear, anger |
| Self-sacrificing | Exploits | Shame, anger |
| Charming | Indifference | Anger |
| Charismatic | Attacks | Guilt, shame |

- Cognitive—Refrain from explaining and intellectualizing. Try to tune into and mention at least one feeling the other person is expressing.
- Needy—Explore the roots of your dependency needs, perhaps with a mental health professional. When you find yourself wanting approval or an indication of affection, use your self-talk (described in the next chapter) to tell yourself that you can survive without this, and give yourself some approval or affection.
- Manipulative—Try to curb your power and control needs; don't always view others as competitors; consciously become more co-operative instead.
- Isolated—Explore the roots of your isolation and try to resolve the issues and unfinished business that are fueling your fears of betrayal and that prevent you from trusting and connecting to others; develop or refine your social skills, make efforts to interact and to socialize.
- Self-absorbed—Become more aware of your behaviors and attitudes that can signal undeveloped narcissism in some areas, such as attention seeking, an entitlement attitude, and lack of empathy; work to reduce the behaviors and attitudes, and to build your healthy adult narcissism. This is explained more extensively in the next chapter.
- Self-sacrificing—Determine what your payoff is for being self-sacrificing, such as gaining admiration, reducing your fear of abandonment, having a lowered sense of self-worth where others are of more importance than you are; work to resolve the root issue, perhaps with a mental health professional.

- Charming—Accept that you cannot charm all of the people all of the time, and that you can be good enough or adequate without their approval. Refrain from continuing to try to use what is not working.
- Charismatic—Use your emotional insulation when attacked by the uptight person, but don't retaliate. Try and determine the roots for your aroused guilt and/or shame, and work to resolve those issues and unfinished business.

You cannot change the uptight person, but you can change yourself to become less vulnerable to having your unpleasant feelings triggered.

You may also find it helpful to understand the possible goal for your relating style. Following are the styles categorized by relating goal:

### Relating Goal(s)—Admiration, Attention, Survival

- Needy
- Charming
- Self-sacrificing

### Relating Goal(s)—Defensive, Protection of Self

- Self-absorbed
- Isolated
- Cognitive

### Relating Goal(s)—Power, Control

- Manipulative
- Charismatic

### OLD PARENTAL MESSAGES

These are the feelings about your self that you consciously incorporated from your parents, or parent figures, beginning at birth; these can play a part in your reactions to the behaviors and attitudes exhibited by the uptight person in your life. You were sent messages about how your parents perceived your lovability, worth, intelligence, looks, talents, and so on. Since many of these have been with you all of your life, you may not be aware of their influences and impact on your responses to others. Remarks, comments, and even nonverbal behaviors, such as how someone looks at you, can trigger those old parental messages, which in turn, trigger your responses that can be either positive or negative: Positive when they are approving and appreciative of your messages, and negative when they are disapproving, show disappointment in you, and/or dislike your messages.

Let's step back and examine what possible old parental messages may be impacting your negative reactions to what others say, do, and/or their attitudes with particular attention to these for the uptight person in your life. Read the items and note which ones seems to carry the most importance for you, and when these are verbalized and/or implied, can anger, infuriate, and/or hurt you.

**Exercise 9.3**
**Lingering Parental Messages**
*Materials*: Two copies of the following scale, several sheets of paper, and a pen or pencil for writing.
*Directions*:

1. Find a place to work where you will not be disturbed. Use one copy of the scale to rate your mother or mother figure, and one copy to rate your father or father figure.

   5–Always or almost always communicated this
   4–Frequently communicated this
   3–Sometimes communicated this
   2–Seldom communicated this
   1–Never or almost never communicated this

| | |
|---|---|
| 1. You never do anything right. | 5 4 3 2 1 |
| 2. You are a disappointment to me. | 5 4 3 2 1 |
| 3. You ought to be ashamed of yourself. | 5 4 3 2 1 |
| 4. You're a mess (or something similar). | 5 4 3 2 1 |
| 5. You're ugly (fat, or something negative about your appearance). | 5 4 3 2 1 |
| 6. How can you be so inept (clumsy, uncoordinated, sing off-key, etc.)? | 5 4 3 2 1 |
| 7. Why can't you be more like (a sibling, cousin, or someone else)? | 5 4 3 2 1 |

8. You're always making mistakes.                          5 4 3 2 1

9. You're not competent.                                    5 4 3 2 1

10. You should have known (better, what I wanted or
    meant, etc.).                                           5 4 3 2 1

2. Take another sheet of paper and make a list of all items rated 3 or higher for both parents so that you have one list of statements. Write the feeling(s) you remember having when you were a child when you heard or sensed these statement from either or both parents.
3. Next, review the list and feelings, and rate the current intensity of the feeling(s) you are experiencing as you read the list and feelings. Rate the current feelings from 0—no intensity, to 10—considerable intensity.
4. Finally, use another sheet of paper and make a list of the statements with current feelings rated 6 or higher. These are the old parental messages that you incorporated on some level; these continue to carry intense feelings for you, and they may, consciously or unconsciously, play a part in your reactions to other people. The uptight person in your life may be doing and/or saying things that you associate with your old parental messages.

## UNDEVELOPED NARCISSISM

A definition and description for self-absorbed behaviors and attitudes were provided in Chapter 1 about the uptight person. These are also known as undeveloped narcissism, where these aspects of one's self remain in an earlier developmental state or phase, such as what would be usually be expected in an infant, child, or adolescent. The self may have developed in some aspects, but not in others, and this can be true for you as well as for the uptight person. You may have fewer aspects of your self that are undeveloped, and other aspects may be more developed than those are for the uptight person, but can still lack some development in other ways. You may have more of the developed healthy adult self with characteristics of empathy, responsibility, creativity, zest for life, an appropriate sense of humor, inspiration, and wisdom. However, your undeveloped aspects may still be playing roles in your reactions to the uptight person in your life.

For example, do you have feelings of hurt, anger, guilt, or shame when the uptight person does or says something that directly or indirectly communicates any of the following about you?

- Attention seeking
- Admiration hungry
- Grandiosity
- An entitlement attitude
- Wanting to be unique and special
- Exploits others
- Arrogant and/or contemptuous
- Lacks empathy
- Shallow emotional life and/or expression
- Lacks self-esteem, or has poor self-esteem
- Violates others' boundaries
- Envious
- Empty at the core of oneself

Your reactions may suggest that you also know or sense a need for more development for this aspect of your self. Just like others who cannot or may not be able to see their aspects of self that are not fully developed, so too may you be unable to see these. You will find it helpful to be open to the idea that you have some undeveloped aspects of self, and work to develop these. Suggestions for development are in the next chapter.

## PSYCHOLOGICAL BOUNDARIES

Important developmental concepts are separation and individuation, and the extent to which these are accomplished plays a significant role in the strength and resiliency of psychological boundaries. Let's define and describe these terms and concepts. Psychological boundaries are defined here as the level and extent to which you perceive yourself as separate and distinct from others; an unconscious understanding of where you end and where others begin. This ending of you is your boundary for your self.

Separation is the condition wherein the child's self becomes differentiated from others, such as from the mother, as a part of expected growth and development. When the expected growth does not occur (and this can happen for a variety of reasons usually out of the control of the child), the person can retain a perception of him/her self as a part of others. This can happen when the parent has significant undeveloped narcissism and the child has to assume responsibility for the welfare and well-being of the parent, which is the reverse of parental nurturing, when the parent is overprotective and/or smothering, or when the parent makes the child responsible for the parent's emotional needs.

Individuation is seen as becoming separate and distinct, and building the self to be a unique and worthwhile individual who makes informed and conscious choices about who and what they want to be as a person. Values, attitudes, beliefs, and the like are not blindly or unconsciously accepted and/or incorporated into the self; these are examined and freely chosen. Thus, the person understands and accepts him/herself as different from all others, recognizes that everyone is unique in some way, and this is a part of psychological boundary strength.

Your psychological boundary strength can play a major role in your reactions to the uptight person, as this person can be a strong sender or projector of negative emotions. When your boundary strength is soft, permeable, or weak in places, you can receive, incorporate, and act on the sent or projected negative emotions. You then have these emotions and have made them your own. Because the sending and incorporating happens on an unconscious level, you remain unaware that you have incorporated, and are acting on, the uptight person's projected feelings. You self-doubts, insecurities, shame, and other feelings can be triggered when you incorporate others' projections, not just those for the uptight person. Some of the intense feelings you experience in interactions with an uptight person could be the result of your taking in that person's projected feelings on top of what you were already feeling, and by doing so you intensify and expand your existing feelings.

Building strong and resilient boundaries requires significant progress in your separation and individuation. You grow in your understanding of just where you end, and where others begin. This may be understood better by examining how you may unconsciously violate others' boundaries by doing some of the following:

- Using others' possessions without first asking permission
- Making plans or obligations that involve another person without consulting him/her

- Entering someone's office or room without knocking and asking or waiting for permission to enter; this includes children's space
- Telling or suggesting what another person should or ought to be or do
- Taking or demanding unearned credit

These are only a few ways that boundaries can be violated, but these are also common violations that, for the most part, are unintentional. You will want to work to reduce and eliminate your violations of others' psychological boundaries.

## CURRENT STATE OF YOUR WELL-BEING

Now that you have some notions about why you react as you do to the uptight person, we'll take a look at the current state of your well-being. Since we all have many dimensions to our self and our lives, we'll take a look at nine aspects; physical, emotional, relational, inspirational, creative, mindful, cognitive, work, and leisure.

*Physical well-being.* Included in this aspect are satisfaction with your weight, eating habits (not over- or under-eating), nutrition, sleep, exercise, compliance with medicine or other treatment, lack of substance abuse such as drugs and/or alcohol, ability to relax, and the like.

*Emotional well-being.* This aspect addresses the range and depth of your emotional experiencing and expression, general everyday mood, ability to experience and express both pleasurable and unpleasant feelings, containing and managing intense emotions for self, and being emotionally present in interactions with others.

*Relational well-being.* This aspect focuses on relationships with others and your satisfaction with the quality of your personal relationships—family, intimate, social, work, and community; and the extent to which you nurture others' growth and development.

*Inspirational well-being.* This transcendent aspect includes having meaning and purpose for your life, awareness of beauty and wonder around you, living by your chosen values, beliefs, morals and ethics; altruistic acts; and feeling connected to the universe.

*Creative well-being.* This refers to the extent to which you incorporate new and novel things and actions into your life. It does not solely refer to special talents, such as music and art, but encompasses all parts of life. Are you satisfied with how you find a better way, improve existing processes, take pleasure in new and novel pastimes and pursuits, and other creative endeavors?

*Mindful well-being.* This aspect addresses the extent to which you are observing and aware of yourself and the world around you. Are you aware of your self in the world as separate and distinct from others, focus on the present and what you do, sense, feel, and experience; do you have awareness of others' emotional states?

*Cognitive well-being.* This aspect refers to the thoughts and ideas you have about your self and about others, affirming your self, you can think clearly, you use your ability to organize and plan activities, you produce new ideas, can think things through before acting, and have wisdom.

*Work well-being.* This aspect, of course, assumes that you work, either in the home or away. It includes time and effort on task(s), visible signs of productivity, quality of productivity, work relationships with boss, peers, subordinates, and if unemployed at this time, plans for future work.

*Leisure well-being.* Restfulness and change of pace characterize this aspect of well-being. Included are recreation, hobbies, and other playful and enjoyable activities.

### Exercise 9.4 Current Well-being

*Materials*: Several sheets of paper and a pen or pencil for writing. The definitions and descriptions given above for aspects of well-being.
*Directions*:

1. Find a place to work where you will not be disturbed that has a suitable hard surface for writing.
2. Begin by reflecting on your current perceptions of your overall well-being. Give this overall perception a rating of 1–extremely dissatisfied to 10–extremely satisfied. Write this number on a sheet of paper.
3. Next, make a list of the aspects of well-being down one side of the paper. For example,

   Physical
   Emotional
   Relational

4. Rate the level of your satisfaction with each aspect using the following scale:

5–Extremely satisfied; 4–Very satisfied; 3–Satisfied; 2–Somewhat dissatisfied; and 1–Extremely dissatisfied.

5. Make another list of the aspects you rated 3 or lower, and identify the parts with which you are most dissatisfied. For example, if you rated Physical as a 3, you could list nutrition, exercise, and eating habits as the parts with which you are most dissatisfied.
6. Review the list you made in step 5 and prioritize each individual part according to its importance for you with your top priority receiving a rating of 1.
7. Take another sheet of paper and write your top five priority items. Place a possible implementation action date beside each, the date when you can take your first step toward becoming more satisfied by taking action to address or remedy it.

Perhaps the most distressing things about having to relate and interact with uptight people are the feelings about oneself that get triggered. This chapter described some possible reasons for the uncomfortable feelings that are aroused, and suggested some short-term strategies that can help reduce some of the negative effects on you. The next chapter continues this discussion and provides additional aspects of self for development, and strategies to cope while you are in the process of becoming more fortified against the projections and other negative behaviors and attitudes of uptight people.

# 10

# Make It Better for Yourself: Coping with the Uptight Person

The most effective coping strategies involve self-development for you to help moderate or eliminate the negative effects of your experiences in the relationship and interactions with the uptight person(s). There are suggestions in previous chapters that address specific behaviors, attitudes, and situations, but most of these are short-term or stopgap strategies. They can get you away from the immediate situation, but do not prevent recurrence of the reactions that you experience. Moderating and/or eliminating the negative reactions and effects on you is the focus and emphasis for this chapter. Addressed are needed perceptual shifts, stress reduction techniques, emotional insulation, managing and containing your intense emotions, building psychological boundary strength, reducing your self-absorbed behaviors and attitudes, and handling others' intense emotions.

## PERCEPTUAL SHIFTS

Each of us has our own unique way of perceiving, but when faced with the uptight person, almost everyone can have perceptions that will get in the way of effectively coping with this person's distressing behaviors and attitudes. Thus, one of the first coping strategies is to make some perceptual shifts where you look at your situation from another angle, which can then lead to your having different reactions, feelings, and thoughts about it, that person, and about yourself. Small shifts can make a big difference. Sometimes the shift is easily accomplished, but many times it can take time and effort before a shift is achieved. When you find that the shift is not complete, or that you are still in the old mind-set, remind yourself of the shift you want to make, and be patient. The shift can be achieved and will work. Shifts you may need to make include the following:

*If you think or feel that you can say or do something that will cause the other person to change:*

**Shift to realizing and accepting that this will not happen, or is an unlikely outcome.**

*If you are trying to get the other person to stop making or causing your unpleasant and uncomfortable feelings:*

**Shift to accepting that you control your feelings, and can choose what to feel.**

*If you expect mutuality in the relationship with an uptight person as he/she is described in this book:*

**Shift to giving up the fantasy of mutuality. This person is so self-absorbed that others exist only insofar that they can meet the self-absorbed person's conscious and unconscious needs. You and others do not exist as separate unique and worthwhile individuals for the person.**

*If you expect that the relationship will become more agreeable and less stressful on you without you having to change:*

**Shift to understanding that lessening the negative effects on you can only be effected in one of three ways:**

- **The uptight person leaves.**
- **You leave.**
- **You change.**

**Although you can have a choice, the most effective choice is often for you to change.**

Let's explore these perceptual shifts a little more. Although you may have had other relationships where you and the other person were able to work out a compromise, this relationship with an uptight person is different because he/she is extremely fearful, anxious, and self-absorbed. What may have worked before with other people will not work now, and you need to realize that your expectations and efforts are futile. It can be difficult to recognize and accept that what you are doing is ineffective, and that being ineffective is increasing your stress and decreasing your self-esteem. You are adding to your distress with this unrealistic expectation. Other people change when they want to change just like you do, and sometimes their connection, respect, and/or affection for you will encourage them to try and change. These kinds of connections, with their positive mutual attributes, are not part of your relationship with the uptight person, who does not have enough respect and/or affection for you to the extent that he/she wants to please you, or to maintain the relationship.

Maintaining a fantasy that you will be able to "cause" the uptight person to change as you wish him/her to change does not allow you to be realistic about your relationship, or to create alternatives for yourself, or to protect your self from that person's negative effects on you. A perceptual shift could allow you to become more content with what you do have and find positive about the relationship, to accept your limitations and recognize your strengths which will fortify you against the uptight person's negative comments, and can provide you with an opportunity to create and seek alternative ways of behaving and relating which can then reduce your frustration.

## YOUR FEELINGS

Other chapters have described how interactions with an uptight person can sometimes, or always, trigger your intense and negative feelings. You may have a perception that the person causes or makes you have these feelings. If you assume the perspective that you control your feelings, this can lead you to understand how and why your feelings are triggered, and how you can block and/or prevent these feelings from becoming triggered. While uptight people can be powerful senders and projectors of their feelings, you don't have to incorporate and take these in, make them a part of your already existing feelings, or awaken your feelings, nor do you have to act on these.

For example, what can unconsciously happen in an interaction could be the following:

- The uptight person feels threatened and this produces a feeling of fear for him/her.
- The fear is too dangerous or overwhelming, so it gets masked with anger.
- The anger is uncomfortable or unacceptable for him/her, and is projected onto the receiver; in this case, that is you.
- You are open and take in the projected anger. If you were already somewhat irritated or annoyed, the projected anger is added to what you are already experiencing, and you then move from irritation to anger. If you were not irritated or annoyed and took in the projected anger, you can then make it yours and you become angry.
- You can then act on the anger without realizing that you took in the projected anger from the uptight person, and are now acting on that.

Resisting taking in others' projections can be difficult, but can also be very beneficial for your emotional well-being. Resistance begins with an awareness and acceptance that you can and do control your feelings. You are not always at the mercy of unseen and uncontrollable forces that you perceive as "causing" your feelings.

The best process to understand your feelings and why these get triggered by others' projected feelings, is to explore some of your past experiences and assumptions, but that is beyond the scope of this book. What can be done here is to increase your awareness of one possibility for how and why your feelings can be triggered. One reason could be transference, which is defined here as an unconscious association of past experiences with current experiencing that has its roots in your family of origin relationships and experiences. Try the following exercise as a sample for identifying possible transference.

**Exercise 10.1**

**Past Experiences**

*Materials*: One or more sheets of paper, a pen or pencil for writing, and a place that has a hard surface for writing where you will not be disturbed.

*Directions*:

1. Sit in silence with your eyes closed, and try to empty your mind. Let your thoughts and feelings go where they will without evaluating or analyzing them; just let them float on the surface of your mind and disappear for the time being. Try to do this for five minutes.

2. When you are ready, open your eyes and think about a person with whom you have a conflict, or who seems to irritate and annoy you, or someone who can say or do things that trigger your feelings of inadequacy or incompetency. Write that person's name at the top of the page, and divide the page into three columns.

3. Label the first column "Behaviors and Attitudes." Then make a list in that column of the specific behaviors and attitudes that describe the person, and annoy you. For each attitude, write what they do or say that exhibits that attitude. For example, if the person displays a superior attitude, and he/she boasts, brags, or plays one-upmanship, you would write those actions to illustrate the attitude. List as many of these behaviors and attitudes as possible.

4. Once the list is complete, label the second column "Mother or Mother figure." Put a check beside each behavior and attitude you listed that is also exhibited by your mother. Label the third column "Father or Father figure" and do the same checking of similar behaviors and attitudes.

5. Review your lists and checks. Take another sheet of paper and write two summary statements. The first statement will be about similarities for behaviors and attitudes of your selected person and your mother. The second statement will do the same for your father.

6. The final step is to read your original list, checkmarks, and your summary statements, and then write an answer to the following question: (you can write as much as you choose): "Could it be that part of my reaction to _____ (name of the person) comes from the past experiences with my mother that, at that time, caused me to have the following feelings about myself (list feelings here)?" Finish the same question about your father. You could now have some understanding of how your unconscious transference could contribute to your current reactions to another person, especially an uptight person.

You may now have a better understanding of why you react as you do, but the most important understanding is that you can control your feelings and not stuff, minimize, or deny these once you can accept that others do not make or cause you to feel as you do. You can have the feelings you do because the other person's actions produced associations for you that you perceive as negative about your self, and/or that is transference involving one or more of your parents. There are many other possibilities for your negative feelings and you are encouraged to explore these with a competent mental health professional who can also guide you to better ways of coping with these when they are triggered.

## THE FANTASY OF MUTUALITY

You probably value mutuality in a relationship, but that has eluded you in the relationship you have with the uptight person. There may be instances where you feel valued and appreciated by this person, but there are many more times when you feel devalued, minimized, unappreciated, inadequate, and so on. Not that you expect that everything will be even or equal, but you do want and expect some mutual respect, acceptance, valuing, and the like as these are the foundations for meaningful, satisfying, and enduring relationships of all kinds.

What can be worse for you is to have an unconscious fantasy that you can achieve mutuality if you work hard enough on the relationship, or change yourself to be more acceptable to the person without losing your individuality or abasing yourself, or that the other person will come to recognize and appreciate you. Fantasies such as these can keep you in an unproductive relationship, cause you to try or to do things that are not in your best interests, and lead to considerable self-dissatisfaction. In addition, your other relationships may also suffer as none of these fantasies will help you with the uptight person, and the negative feelings you have about that failure can be displaced on other relationships.

Do uptight people ever value others? Most likely they do, but only when the other person meets their exacting standards for what others should and ought to be and do. Don't forget that many of their expectations and exacting standards are unconscious on their part, and they do not recognize the impossibility of what they are asking of others such as the following:

- Understanding and acceptance of their perspective without question
- Others' behavior should be in accord with their spoken, unspoken, and unconscious perspectives
- Others should give constant and continual acknowledgment of their superiority, and be attentive and admiring of them
- Others must never have or verbalize an idea, opinion, suggestion, and the like that differs from theirs
- Others should empathize with them, but should not expect reciprocity
- Others should not voice any complaints or disappointments
- There is an expectation that others should expect and accept being exploited by them
- Others should never want or need anything from them

The conscious and unconscious world of uptight people precludes them from mutuality in relationships.

## THE OPTION FOR YOU CHANGING

You're probably wondering why all of the change is up to you, and fretting about the unfairness of this. Let's first assume that you want or have to maintain a relationship with the uptight person. This may be because of personal standards such as when the relationship is marriage and you do not want to consider divorce, or because it is advantageous for you to remain in the relationship, such as a job or work relationship. Your reasons are your own, and as such, are reasonable and valid for you. You have made a decision to stay in the relationship. However, you still want to lessen the negative effects on you. As noted before, there are options; the uptight person leaves the relationship, you leave the relationship, or you change since there is scant or really no reason to believe that the uptight person will change since they have the deeply held conviction that they are right. Hopefully, you have either given up the fantasy that you can say or do something to cause the uptight person to change or to want to change, or you are well on your way to giving up the fantasy. The uptight person changing is one option for the relationship that is most likely to never happen. If you choose to not leave the relationship, you are left with one of two other options; the uptight person leaves, or you change your perceptions about yourself, the relationship, and the uptight person.

The remainder of the chapter presents suggestions for how you can change to lessen the negative effects of the uptight person's behavior and attitudes on you. These are presented in an order to first provide some symptom relief, with distress tolerance techniques and how to emotionally insulate your self. The next set of suggestions and coping skills focus on your understanding of your reactions and your self. Presented are techniques and strategies to help you understand and cope with your triggered emotions, and the importance of developing stronger and more resilient psychological boundary strength to prevent being wounded or feeling discounted. Attention is also given to showing you how to reduce personal self-absorbed behaviors and attitudes that can be negatively affecting your other relationships, of which you are oblivious. The final presentation provides suggestions for handling intense emotions of others, such as when the uptight person "goes ballistic," has a "hissy fit," gets in your face, and so on.

## POSITIVE PERSONAL CHANGES

The positive personal changes presented are:

- Stress reduction
- Emotional insulation
- Managing difficult emotions
- Building psychological boundary strength
- Reducing self-absorption
- Letting others have their emotions

## STRESS REDUCTION

There is considerable evidence that prolonged stress can have significant negative effects on your physical, psychological, and relational well-being. For example, physical conditions such as hypertension and gastrointestinal distress can be caused and/or exacerbated by prolonged stress; as are psychological effects such as anxiety, depression, and panic attacks; and relational effects such as marital discord and frequent conflicts with co-workers and friends. Thus, it is reasonable to expect that the discomfort and discord aroused in a continual relationship with an uptight person could produce stress-related symptoms for you. Complete the following scale to get some idea about the parts of you and your life that can be suffering from stress. After the scale, some stress reducing strategies will be described.

**Exercise 10.2**

**Stress Signals**

*Materials*: A copy of the scale, and a pen or pencil

*Directions*: Rate your experiencing of each item at the current time using the following scale:

5–Continual or almost continual
4–Very frequently
3–Frequently
2–Seldom
1–Never or almost never

| | |
|---|---|
| 1. Difficulty with sleep (too much, too little, interrupted) | 5 4 3 2 1 |
| 2. Over- or under-eating | 5 4 3 2 1 |
| 3. Lack of time or desire for hobbies, recreation, and the like | 5 4 3 2 1 |
| 4. Accept fewer socializing opportunities | 5 4 3 2 1 |
| 5. More frequent conflicts, disagreements, and the like with family, friends, and/or intimate partners | 5 4 3 2 1 |
| 6. Forget important dates, appointments, and/or responsibilities | 5 4 3 2 1 |
| 7. Lose important and necessary items | 5 4 3 2 1 |
| 8. Increased headaches, stomach aches, and/or intestinal distress | 5 4 3 2 1 |
| 9. Reduced zest, joy, or meaningfulness for life | 5 4 3 2 1 |
| 10. Usual tasks and/or assignments are chores to be endured | 5 4 3 2 1 |
| 11. More easily angered, irritated, and the like than is usual | 5 4 3 2 1 |
| 12. Using alcohol, medication, or other drugs more than is usual | 5 4 3 2 1 |

Scoring: Add your ratings and use the following as indications of current stress

49–60: Considerable signs of stress

37–48: Many signs of stress

25–36: Frequent signs of stress

12–24 Some signs of stress

If your score is 30+, you may want to pay particular attention to the stress reduction techniques and strategies that follow. In addition, you can also use the discussion of emotional insulation, boundary strength, and managing and containing intense emotions presented later in this chapter to help reduce the effects of stress on you.

### Stress Reduction Strategies

Stress moderation techniques described here are breathing and sensory distracters. Relaxation procedures, and movement such as dance, exercise, yoga, and so on, are other stress reducers that you can try, but are not presented.

### Exercise 10.3

### Breathing

*Directions*: Find a place where you will not be disturbed, with comfortable seating. Once you become comfortable with breathing exercises, they can be performed anywhere at any time. For the present, it is helpful to be alone in a place free from distractions and disruptions. Turn off phones, televisions, and the like. You may also want to have a clock or timer available. Read all of the procedure before beginning the exercise.

*Procedure:*

1. Sit in silence with your eyes open or closed.
2. Become aware of your breathing, and note its pace—fast, slow, snorting, and so on.
3. Note if your breath seems to be labored, if you are breathing through your nose or through your mouth, or if your breath is easy.
4. Note where your breath seems to originate: your upper chest, diaphragm, or stomach.

5. Now, consciously try to slow your breath and have it come from deep within your chest, and make it slow, deep, and even. Become aware of how your body feels when you do this.
6. If you feel your breath changing back to being fast, labored, and so on, just consciously focus on making it slow, deep, and even.
7. Begin with trying to make your breath slow, deep, and even for one minute, and work up to doing this for five to ten minutes. Note how you feel when you can control your breathing; such as feeling calm, in control, having clearer thoughts, and the like.

## Sensory Techniques

Sensory techniques can be visual, auditory, taste, olfactory, or tactile. All refer to experiencing something through the senses that is pleasant and brings about a feeling of well-being where you are at ease, and do not feel threatened or in danger. When encountering stress, especially prolonged stress, it can be helpful to use one or more of your sensory techniques when you feel stressed, or just as a part of your daily routine. The following exercise is intended to help you develop your personal set of sensory stress reducing techniques.

## Exercise 10.4

### Sensory Savors

*Materials*: Five 3 × 5 or 5 × 8 lined index cards, a pen or pencil, and a sheet of paper
*Directions*: Find a place to work where you will not be disturbed. This exercise can be completed at one sitting, or you can do it at various times. However, it is important for you to complete all sections.

1. Card 1—Visual Pleasures
   Label the card Visual Pleasures. Sit with your eyes closed and allow images to emerge of objects, actions, people, plants, animals, and so on that you find beautiful or pleasurable to see. Examples of visual savors could include items like kittens, a child's smile, a clean and uncluttered desk, fruit piled up at the grocery store, a favorite painting, and so on. List all of the images that emerge for you on this card.
2. Card 2—Auditory Soothers
   Take another card and label it Auditory Soothers. List all sounds you find soothing. Examples could include sounds like waves at

a beach, classical music or the music of your choice, the voice of a loved one, birds singing, and so on. This is the list of your auditory pleasures.

3. Card 3—Taste Delights

    Label the third card Taste Delights and list all the tastes, such as specific foods, that you find comforting, soothing, and satisfying. If you have a medical condition that prohibits any or some of your taste delights, such as what happens with food allergies, also list the substitutes for your comforting taste delights.

4. Card 4—Smell Enhancers

    Label the fourth card Smell Enhancers, and list all of the odors you find pleasurable and soothing. Examples could include bread baking, clean laundry, fresh soap as you lather up, and lotion.

5. Card 5—Touch Calming

    Label the last card Touch Calming, and list all of the things you like to touch and feel. Examples could include silk fabric, smooth stones, and carved beads.

Review all five cards and become aware of the many resources you may have at your disposal that will help reduce your stress or distress. Keep your cards to review periodically, add more savors and distress-relieving measures as you think of them, and resolve to use one of more of these every day, and/or when something about the uptight person in your life distresses you.

## EMOTIONAL INSULATION

Constant interaction with an uptight person can be distressing and leave you in turmoil. Added to this can be your frustration at not being able to effect any positive changes, where nothing you do or say seems to make any difference in the person's behavior or attitude toward you. These interactions become more and more painful to endure, and you can find yourself in a continual state of apprehension and dread of having to interact with that person.

It can be helpful to employ some emotional insulation as a preventive when anticipating interactions with an uptight person. Less effective, but still helpful, is to use this when you did not anticipate an interaction, but while in the interaction you become aware of feeling distressed. It can still work, but is less effective because you did not employ it until there was already some distress. You will still have to deal with your triggered distress, but you do prevent your distress from becoming worse at the point where you begin to use your emotional insulation. The following exercise will guide you to develop your unique emotional insulation. You can use this both as a prevention and also when you have not anticipated and are in the middle of distress.

**Exercise 10.5**

**Emotional Insulation**

*Materials*: A sheet of paper and a set of crayons, felt markers, or colored pencils for drawing

*Procedure*: Find a place to work with a flat surface for drawing, and which is free from distractions and interruptions.

1. Sit in silence for a minute and try to clear your mind of thoughts, feelings, worries, and the like.
2. You can close your eyes for this step, or leave them open. Think about and visualize a barrier between you and another person that allows that person's words to get through and be heard, but also blocks their projected feelings from getting through to you. What does that barrier look like? Open your eyes and draw the barrier you visualized, providing as many details as possible. This is your external emotional insulation that you can use whenever you anticipate an interaction with an uptight person, or are in an interaction and you start to feel distressed.
3. Close your eyes again and visualize a barrier inside you that would keep your feelings from becoming triggered and causing you distress. For example, a barrier could be a steel wall that pushes the feelings to the side, or a train that carries them away for the present. Any barrier that would prevent you from experiencing the distressing feeling in the moment can be used, especially when you are in an interaction with the uptight person. This is your internal emotional insulation. Open your eyes and draw this barrier.
4. Look at what you drew for a barrier, and practice quickly visualizing it without closing your eyes. Allow the external emotional insulation barrier to come into your mind with as much detail as possible. Look at your drawing, if that will help fix it in your mind, until you can quickly visualize it in detail without looking

at it. Then, practice doing the same for your internal emotional insulation.

## MANAGING AND CONTAINING YOUR EMOTIONS

Using emotional insulation can allow you to manage and contain your emotions for the current moment, but won't do anything to help you understand your triggers for these emotions and how to keep these from becoming activated, or how to eliminate them. Many people are just content with denying, rationalizing, repressing, or using other such defense mechanisms as a means to moderate their current emotional experiencing. It can be helpful to better understand what past personal experiences contribute to your current triggers. For example, do you have something that irritates you no matter who says or does it, but you don't know why it irritates you? Or, do you get upset by something that others just brush off, and you don't know why you get upset? In addition, you may find it difficult or impossible to manage and contain the irritation or being upset no matter how hard you try to control it. The process described under "Self-reflective and self-exploration process" in chapter 9 can provide short-term guidance for managing and containing emotions, and provide some space so that you can explore your associations and root causes for why you feel as you do so as to eliminate or reduce intense and negative feelings.

## BUILD PSYCHOLOGICAL BOUNDARY STRENGTH

The extent to which you consciously and unconsciously recognize that you are separate and distinct from others, and they are separate and distinct from you, delineates your boundary strength. Possessing strong and resilient boundaries will be extremely useful to help cope with the negative impact of the uptight person on you in many of the following ways:

- Moderating the extent to which you accept personal responsibility for the well-being of others who are capable of taking care of themselves
- Recognizing and accepting your limits and your strengths
- Having the ability to say no and stick to it

- Resisting manipulation and control by other people
- Developing the ability to reach out and touch others in a meaningful way without becoming vulnerable to their power and control
- Being empathic without becoming enmeshed or overwhelmed with other's feelings, or losing the sense of yourself as separate and distinct from that person
- Behaving in ways that demonstrate your deep understanding of being separate and distinct with respect for others as being separate and distinct
- Recognizing when others are trying to or have succeeded in violating your boundaries, and taking steps to prevent or immediately remediate any violation
- Resisting being persuaded to do things that you do not want to do, or that are not in your best interests
- Controlling any tendency you may have to catch others' emotions, and making conscious choices for who you let in and/or become intimate with so that your acts are more voluntary and informed choices

These are some of the benefits of building your psychological boundary strength. Doing so will also help you resist and screen out many of the negative and distressing projections of the uptight person because you will be better able to define what is yours and what is theirs.

Although the uptight person can be very powerful and forceful, you contribute to your own distress by the level and extent of your psychological boundary strength. Following are some behaviors, thoughts, and characteristics for categories of psychological boundaries that may describe yours. Read these to see which best fits you where you are at this time.

## Soft Psychological Boundary Strength

- Feel that other's well-being and welfare are more important and urgent than yours, even when they are capable of self-care
- An inability to say no and stick to it
- Constantly doing what others want you to do in order to be liked and approved of by them
- Think that you have too much empathy, and are constantly overwhelmed or enmeshed in others' feelings

## Spongy Psychological Boundary Strength

- Subject to being manipulated to do things you do not want to do, or that are not in your best interests
- Can resist or screen out others' projected feelings some of the time, but frequently become enmeshed or overwhelmed by these
- Accept some of your limitations and responsibility for others, but can still find that you do too much for them that they could and/or should do for themselves
- Feel that others take advantage of your good nature

## Rigid Psychological Boundary Strength

- Fear becoming manipulated and/or having to take care of others so much that you keep others at a distance and avoid intimacy
- Seldom, if ever, can be empathic with anyone
- Mistrust almost everyone, or everyone, so that genuine contact is not made or encouraged
- Can feel isolated, excluded, and/or alienated

The best I can do at this point is to make you aware of how you may be contributing to your own distress when interacting with the uptight person. To gain strong and resilient boundary strength requires considerable self-exploration, self-understanding, and self-development. Personal growth of this kind can be accomplished in a variety of ways, and working with a competent mental health professional is one that is helpful by providing guidance, encouragement, and support. This growth can be difficult, and is sometimes painful, but is well worth the time and effort. The short-term strategies presented in this book, such as emotional insulation and stress reduction strategies, can be helpful until you have an opportunity to build strong and resilient boundaries.

### REDUCE SELF-ABSORPTION

Chapter 2 also addresses this topic, but is focused on the uptight person. Just as that person is not aware of these attitudes and behaviors, so too are you unaware of some of yours. What follows is an attempt to increase your awareness of some of your possible self-absorbed behaviors and attitudes. As you read these, become aware of how you exhibit the behavior or thought, and/or if you have received comments or feedback about these You can rate the frequency, if that will be helpful: 5–always or almost always, 4–frequently, 3–sometimes, 2–seldom, or 1–never or almost never.

## Attention-seeking behaviors

- Talk loudly, and/or frequently interrupt others, and/or finish other people's sentences
- When talking with others, you change the topic to focus on you in some way
- Make noisy and/or grand entrances and exits

## Admiration hungry behaviors

- Boast and/or brag
- Engage in self-nominations for awards and other recognitions
- Fish for compliments/flattery

## Grandiosity

- Tend to take on too many commitments and tasks
- Exaggerate everything about yourself, such as accomplishments
- Never admit mistakes, lapses, errors, and so on
- Can be arrogant and contemptuous

## Impoverished ego

- Feel deprived and taken advantage of by others
- Continually point out how you are treated unfairly and unjustly
- Focus on and emphasize the negatives in your life

## Entitlement Attitude

- Expect preferential treatment and become angry when you don't get it
- Ignore rules, laws, policies, and so on
- Become profoundly disappointed when you don't receive what you want, expect or feel is rightfully yours

## Unique and special

- Expect constant and continual compliments and affirmations of your uniqueness
- Demand recognition of your superiority
- Dress and act to be recognized as unique and special

## Emptiness

- Feel that others are happy or have something positive that you do not have
- Excessively engage in activities
- Use drugs and/or alcohol excessively to keep from relating and feeling

## Envy

- Feel that others have what you should have, and they don't deserve it—you do
- Feel that others get the recognition and rewards that are rightly yours
- Feel that others have an unfair advantage, or are part of a network, and your assets and contributions are minimized

## Extensions of self

- You demand that others do things for you that you could do for yourself
- Enter others' space without asking or waiting for permission
- Touch others without their permission
- Use others' possessions without asking permission

## Lack of empathy

- Fail to recognize what others are feeling
- Say and do insensitive things that demean and devalue others and are unaware of the impact of what you say or do has on the other person
- Your responses in interactions do not acknowledge others' feelings

- You understand the words for feelings, but don't experience the feelings

## Shallow emotions

- You do not experience or express levels and graduations of feelings
- Fear and anger are the only emotions you express
- Grief, loss, happiness, and so on are foreign to you and are not experienced or expressed

## Inappropriate sense of humor

- Taunt, tease, and/or are sarcastic
- Make fun of others' inadequacies, deficiencies, frailties, and the like
- Tell demeaning, ethnic, racist, and sexist jokes

## Exploit others

- Take advantage of others' ignorance, and/or their good nature for your personal gain
- Lie, or cheat, or steal, and so on
- Misuse your status, role, power, or position for personal gain

After you increase your awareness of some of your self-absorbed behaviors and attitudes, you can take another step to consciously reduce some, eliminate some, work to understand others and their antecedents, and attempt to maintain and expand your awareness of other such behaviors and attitudes you may have. It is also helpful to allow yourself to become aware of the negative impact these are having on others you care for in your relationships.

## OTHERS' INTENSE EMOTIONS

The final topic, handling others' intense emotions, is especially important when you have to interact with an uptight person on a regular or continual basis, as these people can be powerful senders of their negative feelings. What can you do in the moment when it is obvious to you that the uptight person is feeing something intensely, which is most all of the time? The longer term strategy of building your self is basic, but this does take time to fully implement so that you can experience the positive outcomes. In the meantime, you still have to interact with the uptight person, and may continue to have difficulty in handling their intense emotions. Following are some short-term strategies:

- Have a clear understanding and acceptance of the limits of your responsibility. You are not responsible for others' feelings just as others are not responsible for your feelings.
- Uptight people can be powerful senders of their emotions, and you need to block these so that you do not incorporate them and make them your feelings. Emotional insulation can help with this.
- Use nonverbal avoidance techniques, such as not looking the person in the eye, turning your body slightly away from the person, and putting a barrier between you such as a table or notebook—anything will work.
- Refuse to allow your feelings to be triggered in the interactions. Deal with these later if needed.
- Do not use humor or change of topic as a distraction. This is likely to infuriate the person and make the situation worse.
- Listen to the person, but only make neutral comments. Don't try giving rational or logical arguments for your perspective; make your answers an acknowledgement of that person's feelings. They are unlikely to hear anything else.
- DO NOT CONFRONT! Confrontation will not work and is likely to make you feel worse.
- Visualize your place of peace and use that visualization during interactions with the uptight person.

Your goals are to stop becoming agitated and having negative feelings about your self triggered. You may also have the added benefits of defusing some of the intensity in the interaction, and of affirming your individuality and separateness when you don't get caught up in the uptight person's intensity and anxiety. While these are limited goals and benefits, they are very important and significant to your well-being, and you will have made great strides in coping with an uptight person when you implement these understandings, awareness, and techniques.

## ENDING THOUGHTS

One intent for the material in this book is to guide you the reader to create personal coping strategies for the uptight people in your life. Having to interact with someone who can be termed uptight is usually very frustrating and upsetting, and these states do not allow you to understand your reactions or initiate effective and constructive coping strategies. It is hoped that the descriptions have increased your understanding of the uptight person, encouraged you to give up efforts to get that person to change, to relinquish the fantasy that you will do or say something that would make them want to change, and have provided you with ways to moderate the negative effects they can have on you. I also hope that you will continue your growth and development, and will reap the benefits for your efforts.

# References

Brown, N. *The destructive narcissistic pattern.* Westport, CT: Praeger, 1992.
*Diagnostic and statistical manual of mental disorders.* 4th ed. Washington, DC: American Psychiatric Association, 2000.


## RESOURCES

BrainPhysics Web site. http://www.brainphysics.com
Brown, Nina. *Coping with infuriating, mean, critical people: The destructive narcissistic pattern.* Westport, CT: Praeger, 2007.
Kernberg, Otto. *Borderline and narcissistic conditions.* New York: Aronson, 1990.
Marra, Thomas. *Depressed & anxious.* Oakland, CA: New Harbinger Publishers, 2004.
Terwilliger, D., and M. Williams. "Obsessive-Compulsive Personality Disorder." BrainPhysics Web site. 2010. http://www.brainphysics.com/oc-personality.php
Williams, M. T. "Obsessive-compulsive personality disorder: When everything has to be just right." OCD Resource Center of Florida Web site. 2009. http://www.ocdhope.com/oc-personality-disorder.php

# Index

.

## About the Author

NINA W. BROWN, Ed.D., is a Professor and Eminent Scholar of Counseling at Old Dominion University in Norfolk, Virginia. She is a Licensed Professional Counselor, a Nationally Certified Counselor, and a Fellow of the American Group Psychotherapy Association. Dr. Brown is the author of 19 published books including *Dead End Lovers*; *Children of the Self-Absorbed*; *Coping with Infuriating, Mean, Critical People: The Destructive Narcissistic Pattern*; *Loving the Self-Absorbed*; and *Coping with Your Partner's Jealousy*.